POWER MARKETING
FOR LUXURY REAL ESTATE

DAVID M. MICHONSKI

For information address The Stonesong Press, 27 West 24th Street, Suite 510, New York, NY 10010-3271.

Printed in the United States of America
Interior design and composition by Brad Walrod/Kenoza Type

First Edition
10 9 8 7 6 5 4 3 2 1

ISBN-10: 1-449-92674-6
EAN-13: 978-1-449-92674-8

www.PowerMarketing.pro

For my wife, Linda, who has the patience to allow me to dream

Contents

Acknowledgments

Over twenty-five years ago, G. Wade Staniar of LandVest in Boston taught me most of the lessons in this book. He spared no one his candor, and I was no exception. In the years since, I have only become more and more grateful, as I know that I have not always taken the time, nor shown the patience, nor sometimes the courage, to be so candid with all my protégés. I wish I had.

John Coburn, Jr., my former partner at LandVest, was this book's first reader. Gifted with the entrepreneur's spirit of freedom and risk taking, he was often exactly what this author needed. I am also indebted to Stephanie Coburn for painstakingly going through the rough first draft and encouraging me to make it better.

Thanks to all my former colleagues at LandVest: Bob Borden, my astute partner on the North Shore of Long Island who made my whole career possible; Chris Burr, who worked with me on Clarendon Court; Jim Retz, who was always a wealth of stories, some of which I have incorporated here.

I thank Bill Andruss of Sotheby's International Realty in Greenwich for reading the first draft and providing his many comments with the gentlemanliness that comes so naturally to him. It was Ellen Scordato of Stonesong Press who provided a much needed "kick in the butt" to abandon prior organization. Her insight added enormously to readability. Pollie Seidel, the manager of the Old Greenwich office of Sotheby's, was an invaluable sounding board and helpful critic. The book is immensely better because of her caring to get it right. Katie Gilligan served as the first copy editor, helping to give the book a sense of order. Lana Bartolot was the editor brave enough to cut a third of the book, making it a quicker read, while my daughter, Katherine, provided the final cuts without any hesitation to tighten her father's thoughts, for which we can all be grateful. Philip Kiracofe did an amazing job of utilizing marketing tools to put the book in front of you, my audience. Finally, I want to thank Glenn Randall, the owner of Clarendon Court in Newport, Rhode Island, for allowing me to photograph his home and put it on the cover.

No book is written without strains on those we love. Mine was no exception. Because I wrote best at the beginning and end of the day, my wife, Linda, was left wondering for too many mornings and too many nights how long it takes to write a book and whether the last chapter would ever get done. Her support, patience and love are embodied in the thirty-three years during which she has continued to take a chance on me.

Introduction

Τ his book is an invitation to join the elite world of agents marketing luxury real estate. By its end you will know how to list and sell luxury real estate in any market at any time and, through *power marketing*, transform yourself into the millionaire's real estate agent.

Power marketing is both a mindset and a series of actions that maximize the chances of competitive bidding for any property.

It is different from the marketing tools you use daily; the local MLS, advertising, promotion and now national websites. *Power marketing* wrenches more buyers out of these tools and focuses on what you need to do with buyers. *Power marketing* addresses the differences in the luxury market and creates competition for luxury properties. It grows out of the unique requirements of a market that is extremely small, where buyers, due to their wealth, do not have to buy. It overcomes their lack of urgency to act. Moreover, by presenting buyers with their competition, *power marketing* actually makes them feel more comfortable to buy and often to bid. It creates an orchestrated moment when many problems associated with reluctant buyers dissolve.

Power marketing is the expertise you should possess before listing a luxury property, certainly long before promoting yourself as a luxury marketer. It should become the essence of your personal marketing message.

Power marketing is based on human nature—and is largely unchanging and not trend-dependent. Once you grasp it, you will own the fastest way I know to sell luxury real estate, and its strategies and successes will be yours for life.

Power marketing is about understanding enough about what drives buyers to act that you, as an agent, actually have the power to influence their actions—and do.

While the luxury market is my focus and laboratory, *power marketing* can empower you to handle the listing and sale of any real estate in any market, at any time. It should dramatically increase your income from the market's every strata.

Best of all, *power marketing* can enable you to become the real estate agent to the millionaires in your market. You can gain entry to an elite arena of movers and shakers, celebrities and CEOs. You will have the most in-demand sales information. You will gain entry to the market where six- and seven-figure commissions are earned and where the prestige that accompanies a luxury sale can lift one's career to star-studded heights. By the end of this book, even the novice can thrive in this exciting world. Come, and let me show you how.

David M. Michonski
Greenwich, Connecticut

1

Learning What to Do (and Why) from an Auction

I t's every real estate agent's dream: a room full of wealthy, intelligent buyers freely, excitedly, even cheerfully straining to pay more.

Where better than an upscale auction to find an example of the competition needed to pay up for an object? I am always mesmerized by the auctioneer, barking and shouting.

"Do I have a starting bid of two million?" he bellows as dozens of buyers wave paddles in the air, enticed by an opening bid way under the likely valuation range of $6 million to $6.5 million.

Pulses start to race.

Within seconds the bidding rises to $2.5M, then $3M, $3.5M, $4M, $4.5M. The competition disables the bargain hunters. Those with the financial might to win take center stage in an exhilarating drama. With so many bidders now clamoring for the same prize, buyers become fearless; initial timidity is overcome by liberated courage to bid high. The comforting presence of multiple buyers provides validation for everyone's desire. Their instinct for bargain hunting vanishes.

"The current bid is four and a half million dollars. Do I hear five million dollars?" The auctioneer's eyes quickly survey the room as his assistants strain to leave no bidder unwatched.

Suddenly, he shouts, "New bidder in the back of the room at five million dollars!" Breathless gasps rise from the audience as heads turn to see who has entered the fray. The new bidder's emergence validates each buyer's belief in the wisdom of their pursuit. The desire to be the victor of the moment takes over and mixes with the desire to stand out among others, and translates into elevated arms and waving paddles. What a sight!

"Do I have five and a half million?"

"Yes!" he yells. "Thank you, madam."

Hearts skip a beat, heads strain, gasps continue in the audience as the bidding goes up and up. With the presence of so many buyers, no one is worried about overpaying.

"Do I have six million? Yes, to the right. Do I hear six and a half? Yes, thank you, sir," he says smiling kindly into the eyes of the latest bidder.

"We have six and a half million dollars. Do I hear seven million?"

Winning is now everything, and in this moment, as the great philosopher Thomas Hobbes noted, the thoughts "are to the desires as scouts and spies, to range abroad and find the way to the things desired..."[1] The power that comes from having money has found its moment. This is what money is for,[2] to get us what we want and not let other mere humans think they can deny us. Moneyed power now rules and our desire for precedence above others is going to be satisfied—and now!

With bids rising above the valuation range, all the exhaustive research into pricing and cataloging to create a defensible value range wafts hazily and indefinitely into the misty heat of momentary rationalization. In this frenzy, buyers are only focused on winning.

The auctioneer, in turn, is focused on creating a market that will determine value, not on getting what the valuation department estimated. Those estimates may be wrong and now are close to meaningless. By filling the room and extracting competitive bids, he has raised the comfort level of everyone to buy. He has created the market conditions under which to extract the highest price. Now his skill at orchestrating the process will create value or add to it. Price is now a function of marketing.

The new bidder in the back of the room raises his paddle and nods to $7 million.

"We have seven million dollars!" shouts the auctioneer excitedly. "Do I have seven and a half million?"

The audience pauses. Heads turn left and right. Eyes then dart around the room searching for who will bid up.

"I have seven million dollars in the back of the room. Do I hear seven and a half million?" he repeats.

Silence, fidgeting, strained necks popping up like submarine periscopes.

"Last call. I have seven million dollars. Going once, going..."

Suddenly a paddle near the front rises.

"We have seven and a half million dollars, ladies and gentlemen. Do I have eight?"

The paddle at the back of the room slowly rises with the buyer's head pushing up from his neck and then a nod of acquiescence.

"I have eight million dollars. Do I have eight and a half million?" The lady up front cautiously raises her paddle yet again.

"I have eight and a half million dollars. Do I have nine million dollars? nine million dollars?" he asks again. "Do I have a bid for nine million dollars?"

The paddle at the back of the room rises. "Ladies and gentlemen, I have nine million dollars at the back of the room. Do I hear nine and a half million?" He smiles down to the lady toward the front. She leans to her right and then to her left. She stares at the object and pauses. Slowly she moves her head negatively ever so reluctantly.

Sensing exhaustion, but pleased that $2 million more was extracted from the room in less than half a minute, the auctioneer quickly does a final scan of the scene and says to all:

"I have nine million dollars. Last call. All bids in. I have nine million dollars. Going once, going twice. SOLD to the gentlemen in the rear for nine million dollars."

An explosion of applause fortifies the buyer's conviction. Satisfaction is in the air.

The auction process crystallizes what agents (and their sellers) wish for in selling real estate: buyers freed from hesitancy, willing to act, eager to pay more than someone else. Auctions provide insight into the human psyche, letting you see that wonderful moment in time when buyers have the urgency to act on a desire you create.

As you read, keep this auction scene in your mind; I will refer back to it throughout the book. To become a great luxury agent, to become a power marketer, you will need to harness and master the auctioneer's ability to create fearless and eager buyers. This is a real estate agent's dream, in this book I will show you how to make it come true.

Let me point out some aspects of the auction to keep in mind for *power marketing* going forward.

Value Bands for Pricing

Long before auction day, the seller of an object takes it to the auction house to be analyzed, researched, and valued. This process is much like a homeowner asking you into a home for a consultation and valuation.

The valuers do not provide an appraisal until they have thoroughly inspected and analyzed the object—much the way you research a comparable market analysis (CMA).

Once the object has been fully researched and documented with data such as past sales, rarity, or celebrity value and comparable offerings, the auction house will determine its condition and adjust the base price up or down accordingly, just as you would with a luxury home.

But unlike you, will they give a price? Not likely.

The valuers don't know the price that item will fetch. Therefore, they provide an estimated range of values that gets printed in the program, and even that is really just an educated guess. They know that value is not determined by valuers, but by markets.

Getting More or Getting Less

Next, they will suggest an appropriate marketing plan to get the highest price within that range, which typically includes creating a brochure and publishing the background or provenance of the object. They will give the value range estimate, engage in target marketing to known contacts, and advertise to unknown buyers. If the object has celebrity or rarity value, they may conduct a publicity campaign. All these marketing steps have one goal in mind: to get as many qualified bidders as possible in the room or on the phone on the day of the auction. If they are successful at getting the bidders together, they will get a higher price. If not, they will get less.

Comfort from Another's Desire

Fast forward to auction day. There's a packed room of buyers with all the attendant anticipation and buzz. As the start draws near, attendees' desire for the acquisition increases with the number of people coming into the room. Ironically, the more buyers who want this object, the more their comfort increases, despite the fact that the more bidders in the room, the higher the price they will pay. To emphasize the importance of raised comfort from the presence of others, consider the opposite.

Sole Buyer Syndrome

What if only one buyer showed up? I call the resulting feeling "sole buyer syndrome." The buyer would probably be wondering why no one else came and would be filled with doubts and questions. The buyer would ask, "Why am I bidding on this when no else is?" These are the same feelings buyers have when they are looking at real estate that has been on the market for a while with no bids and they are the sole buyer.

Sole buyers are nervous because others are not present to validate their good sense and judgment. And without that validation, is any buyer going to bid aggressively for an object? Not likely.

Securing that validation is the initial goal of a good marketer. We do that by filling the room, generating comfort for each participant by the presence of others.

The auctioneer then augments this comfort-raising strategy with a low opening price, followed by the most valuable comfort-raising action: the large number of buyer paddles at the opening bid.

The number of raised hands in the room makes potential bidders feel confident, provides confirmation of the buyers' desire, and validates each buyer's individual sense of good taste. Moreover, it induces competition and want. It is the want that now sets the value; the greater the number who want something, the greater its perceived worth.

> The more people who want something, the greater the percevied worth.

Moving the Audience Up in Price

What happens next is a quick judgment call by the auctioneer as to the size of the increments for raising the bidding, based upon the number of buyers in the audience. The increments must be small enough to retain the existing bidders and bring in new buyers, all the while advancing the price steadily. The psychology of the auction is one in which buyers always believe that just one more small bid will secure them the prize.

New bidders are encouraged by the number of others who want this object. Every great auctioneer focuses on raising the comfort level of buyers to bid. He controls the psychology of the sale to loosen the buyer's grip on their wallets and liberate higher bids. When he does so, the sense of value is surrendered to the desire to win and the comfort of being part of but still the head of the pack.

Price Is Now a Function of Marketing

Unlike in the real estate industry, where agents try to achieve the asking price, here the auctioneer focuses on marketing—not the research or valuation department's estimates. He understands that price is a function of his marketing efforts during the live auction.

The Public Nature

There is one other marketing principle at work in this scenario—this is a public bidding process where the ability to see the other buyers raising their hands helps cement the desire to win. That there is plenty of demand for this object is visible to everyone in a highly public way. The auctioneer does not shy from the public aspect; he encourages it.

The Heat of the Auction

As the bids continue, it is up to the auctioneer to determine how much is left in the buyers' pockets. This expertise is what the seller hired the auctioneer to deploy.

New bidders liven the auction. They may have intended to bid, but were waiting to see how high bids were going before stepping in. The process will likely reduce to two bidders who will go back and forth until one is exhausted. But what is important is the ability of the auctioneer to create multiple simultaneous bidders out of which will emerge the highest price this market can bear. This is *power marketing*.

The Last Call

The most important final maneuver by the auctioneer comes just as the auction looks like it is winding down and bids are trailing off, the "last call." He alerts everyone that they have one final chance to bid higher. and threatens to close down the process. As a result, the auction reignites and suddenly an additional two million dollars of value is unleashed just by announcing the last call to the buyers.

By the end of the auction, the auctioneer has conducted a symphony of orchestrated emotions and desires towards a crescendo of positive feelings. The buyer feels good about the fairness of the process, that so many others wanted the object and most importantly, about winning. The seller is satisfied to have gotten the highest price a true market will pay while the auctioneer can rest knowing a real market was created.

The Takeaway

The auction provides an outstanding example of key *power marketing* concepts.

- *The goal of power marketing:* competition from multiple bidders vying simultaneously for an object.
- *Fill the room:* all initial marketing intends to "fill the room" with many potential buyers, not to find just one.
- *Awareness:* the presence of other buyers disables bargain hunting and dispels fear, actually raising comfort and liberating buyers to act.
- *"Sole buyer syndrome:"* being the sole buyer increases hesitancy to act and can be overcome only by the presence of other buyers.
- *Validating belief and desire:* multiple buyers validate desire and belief in the wisdom of bidding, unleashing each other emotionally and psychologically to buy.
- *Winning:* the desire to win among competitive successful and wealthy buyers can become everything, sometimes even surpassing value considerations.
- *Never set prices:* auctioneers never provide a selling price; just reasonable and thoughtful guesses as to the likely range within which an object will sell.

- *Price is a function of marketing:* price is determined by markets, not valuers (or real estate agents). What something is worth is determined by the number of people who want it and the marketer's skill at orchestrating that desire.

- *Comfort releases value:* the more comfortable buyers become, the more value is unleashed.

- *Value creation:* good marketing skills add value to the object and form part of the value being released.

- *Power marketing* is the ultimate value-added marketing.

- *The last call:* making the last call can add 5 percent to 20 percent more to the final selling price.

- *True value: power marketing's* competition determines the true value of a property, whether it is below or above the listed price.

2

Luxury Real Estate and the Market for It

Your initial *power marketing* task is to fill the hypothetical room as in our auction story. You cannot do so without first determining the size of the target market you are inviting in. This requires defining luxury real estate and learning how it differs from ordinary residential real estate.

The "Million Dollar and Up" Definition

It used to be that luxury real estate had a clear cut-off point: properties valued at a million dollars and more. People associate "million dollar" with "millionaire" and that connotes luxury and quality. While the definition today can no longer be so simple, for the purposes of the next few pages, let's just stick to that definition: million-dollar-and-up properties = luxury real estate.

How Big is the "Million Dollar and Up" Market?

One person who has tried to shed light on the issue is Zhu Xiao Di, a researcher at the Joint Center for Housing Studies at Harvard University. In 2004, he issued a study titled "Million-Dollar Homes and Wealth in the United States."[3] Using the million-dollar benchmark as a dividing line, he tried to calculate how many luxury homes exist and who owns them.

THE RICH AND THE WORLD INSIDE THE GATE

Who are the luxury buyers?

At first glance, the market I address in this book would seem to be large and growing—the wealth beyond the gate is breathtaking.

Capgemini and Merrill Lynch published a book titled, *Wealth: How the World's High Net Worth Individuals Grow, Sustain and Manage Their Fortunes.*[9] It documents the trends of the rich and is well worth a brief review. Here's a quick takeaway.

High Net Worth Individuals (HNWIs) are those with $1 million in investable assets, excluding their primary residence. A more elite class called Ultra-HNWIs are individuals with $30 million in investable assets, excluding their primary residence.

In 1996 HNWIs numbered about 6 million worldwide. Ten years later their ranks had swelled to nearly 10 million. This "explosively expanding class of individuals" is experiencing both unit growth (the number of individuals) and volume growth (their wealth), a highly positive combination for any market.[10]

HNWIs controlled approximately $17 trillion in 1997. By 2007 they controlled $37 trillion-more than double in ten years. In this ten-year period some $20 trillion in assets was newly created and is now owned by HNWIs. Another way of looking at it: their investable assets increased on average by $20 million each and they each had on average $37M (again, excluding the value of their primary residence). Money keeps flowing to the few at the top and they have increasingly deeper pockets from which to spend on luxury real estate.

New Money = New Opportunity

New money is gaining impressively over old money. The book *The Millionaire Next Door* notes that 90 percent of the millionaires in the United States made their money during their lifetime, while only 10 percent inherited it.[11] This means that the luxury housing market will be increasingly fueled by new money, not old money; and that the market is open for new blood—your new blood.

Another point: emerging markets are likely to outperform the rest of the world. The GDP growth of emerging markets such as Brazil, Russia, India, and China exceeds that of mature markets. In the case of India and China, growth has been double that of mature economies. Much of this new wealth will make its way into your local luxury market.

Number of HNWIs Versus the General Population (Worldwide as of 2006)

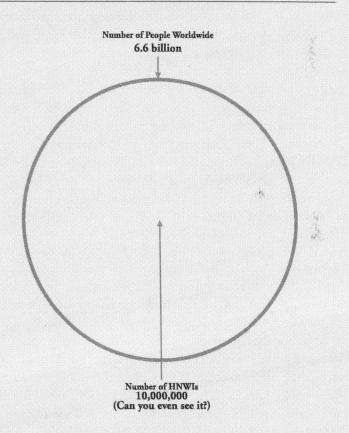

Number of People Worldwide
6.6 billion

Number of HNWIs
10,000,000
(Can you even see it?)

> While wealth seems to be concentrated and skyrocketing it is also increasingly diversified ethnically and culturally. This means that as the old money burns out, is depleted, and divided among heirs, your marketing will have to be even more international and more targeted to those with the new money. It also means that the luxury world will increasingly be open to a more diverse group of agents. Why shouldn't it include you?
>
> What we now want to know is "How big is the target market that our seller-clients hire us to access?" We need to know how many of those HNWIs and Ultra HNWIs buy luxury homes.
>
> What we are about to find out is that it is far smaller than most people imagine.

Zhu noted that there have been two attempts to determine the number of million-dollar homes. One attempt by the Census Bureau concluded that there were 313,759 million-dollar or more homes in the country in 2000.[4]

Unfortunately, the data set was flawed. First, in the 2000 Census not everyone was asked the same question. This meant that the 2000 Census number was an estimate instead of an actual figure: "This estimate may vary from the actual values because of sampling variation or other factors."[5] Second, the Census limited itself to single-family homes; it did not include the tens of thousands of million-dollar-plus condominiums and cooperatives in high-end areas. Third, the 2000 Census counted only primary residences in the tally, leaving out the many second and even third or fourth million-dollar homes.

Finally, the Census data was inaccurate because it excluded any town with fewer than 100,000 people. As a result, it omitted Beverly Hills, Palm Beach, Greenwich, Gross Pointe, and the innumerable other small enclaves of wealth that form the backbone of the luxury real estate market. Because of this undercounting, the 313,759 figure is lower than the actual circumstances.

A second source of data Zhu looked at is the Survey of Consumer Finances (SCF), which is done by the Federal Reserve every three years.[6] The SCF reports that in 2001 there were about 850,000 households in the United States that owned primary residences worth at least $1 million, nearly three times the figure determined by the Census and a difference of 536,241 households.

Zhu concluded, "Exactly where the actual number of 'million dollar' homes owned as primary residences lies in between these estimates [and] is impossible to calculate."[7]

While it may be impossible to calculate with any precision, we know enough from this inconclusive data to draw some fundamental conclusions. For the million-dollar-and-up price range, it is enough to know what percentage of the over-

Money keeps flowing to the few at the top and they have increasingly deeper pockets from which to spend on luxury real estate.

all population is likely to be buyers or sellers. With this data, we can then gauge the overall size of the market and, from a probability point of view, gauge what it takes to hit it.

Calculating the "Million Dollar and Up" Percentage of the Whole: Two Views

If we were to take the 313,759 homes the 2000 Census claims are million-dollar-and-up and divide this number by the fifty-five million single-family owner-occupied homes the Census determined, we find that the million-dollar-and-up market is 0.6 of 1 percent of the whole.

A second percentage comes from looking at the whole market through the SCF claim of 850,000 million-dollar homes. If we similarly divide that number by the 70 million owner-occupied housing units[8] that existed in 2001, we still get a small percentage—just 1.21 percent of all homes. (Remember that if Zhu is right, this 850,000 number is overestimated.)

From the above we at least know that in 2000–2001 the number of U.S. million dollar homes ranged somewhere between 0.6 percent and 1.21 percent of the total of all owner-occupied housing units.

Believing one figure is too low and the other is too high, let's average the two. By doing so, we can reasonably determine that the million dollar and up market consists of 0.9 of 1 percent of the market. Let's just call it "less than 1 percent" of all housing units. That is good enough for our purposes.

Our working definition for luxury real estate when defined as "million dollar and up" is "less than 1 percent" of the whole US housing market.

Estimated Luxury Market Using the Million Dollar and Up Definition

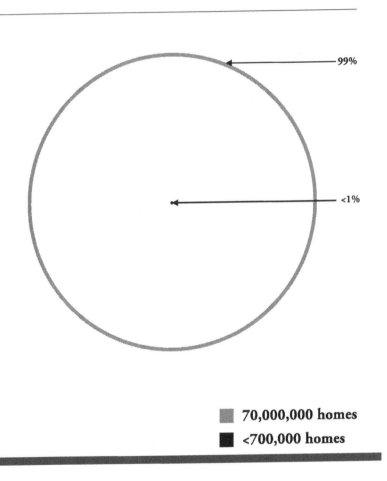

99%

<1%

■ 70,000,000 homes
■ <700,000 homes

The Top 10 Percent Definition

For many years in the luxury marketing business, the term "million dollar and up" was a sufficient definition of luxury real estate. But what about markets like Marin and Sonoma Counties in California; or Palm Beach and Beverly Hills; or Manhattan or Greenwich, where the average sale is over $2 million and 74 percent of all sales in 2010 were over $1 million? In Palm Beach and Beverly Hills $1 million will probably not even buy a building lot, let alone a luxury property. Million-dollar homes in these markets are as ordinary as ranch houses in a 1950s subdivision.

Number of Luxury Homes in US Using the Top 10 Percent Definition

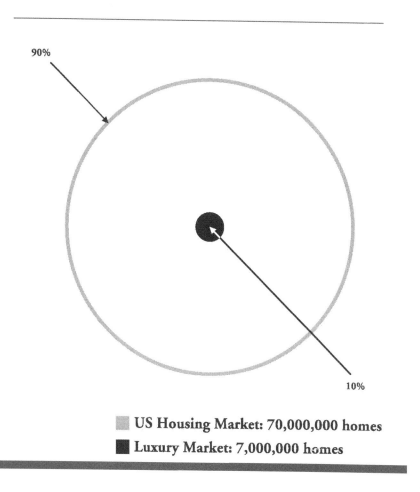

90%

10%

US Housing Market: 70,000,000 homes
Luxury Market: 7,000,000 homes

Clearly, the real estate industry needs new guidelines to measure where the luxury market begins and the ordinary ends. Let's therefore see how we can improve on the "million dollar and up" definition.

Years ago the grand lady of all luxury real estate marketing firms, Previews (founded in 1933 and bought by Coldwell Banker in 1980), suggested defining the luxury market as the top 10 percent of any market. That's been upheld by more recent books dealing with the sector. Defining luxury real estate as a percentage versus a fixed value at least addresses the markets that have properties valued at less than that $1M fixed value.

While the "top 10 percent" definition helps include lesser valued properties, it defines the class so expansively that it actually dilutes the very market we are trying to define. Using our current data, if, as the Census says, there are 50 million single family owner-occupied homes, or, if, as SCF says, there were 70 million owner-occupied housing units, then using the "top 10 percent" definition, there are five and a half to seven million homes that make up the luxury real estate market. Suddenly, the 10 percent definition has increased the highest government estimate of 850,000 by nine times. Utilizing the 10 percent definition overestimates by so much as to trivialize it.

Moreover, if a market has very narrow pricing parameters, the definition may not work at all. For instance, let's say we have a market where homes range in price from $300,000 to $600,000. According to the "top 10 percent" definition, the homes from $540,000 to $600,000 are the luxury properties. Is the difference between luxury and not luxury only $60,000? Probably not. It is even possible that there really are no luxury properties in this market—no definition should try to include them.

The "top 10 percent" definition also does not account for uniqueness. After all, in the example above, how much more special is the $600,000 property that falls within the definition than the $540,000 property that does not? The same holds true for markets with a plethora of $1M to $2M homes. If we define luxury property as the top 10 percent of those markets, it means that only homes from $1.8M to $2M qualify. This may or may not be the case. Using this definition a lot of million-dollar-and up homes get left out and a lot of $500,000 to under $1 million homes are included.

The value of using something like the "top 10 percent" definition is that it acknowledges the limitations of using a set price point definition such as "million dollar and up." For example while a $1,500,000 two-bedroom apartment in Manhattan is unlikely to be a luxury property, the same priced property in Austin, Texas, or Burlington, Vermont, may very well be the epitome of luxury real estate. Using a percentage of a market as a definition allows the definition to adapt to various and often quite different markets. I want to try to preserve that flexibility. Let's therefore build on this insight.

Toward a New Definition

I define a luxury property as two to three times the average price of all homes in a particular geographic market. In my own experience I have found it useful to use the higher multiple, such as three times the average price, for markets where average prices are low. In mature luxury markets where average prices are high, I use the lower multiple of two. I strongly urge that the definition not fall below two times the average price and it is impractical for it to go above three times. Whatever multiple you choose apply it consistently over the years during which you study and operate within your market. For the purpose of this book, I will use two and a half times average price.

Why this starting point? First, the type of luxury property discussed in this book is anything but average. It should be above average by some significant multiple.

In this case, it must be two to three times an average price of a home to ensure that the properties encompassed by this definition are indeed rare. This definition guarantees that the properties it defines

Luxury real estate = two to three times the average price in a market + requisite qualities.

are "luxury" and sit at the top of the market. In this way my definition offers the same flexibility as the top 10 percent model; it too accounts for fluctuations in various markets. But unlike the top 10 percent model, some markets, based upon this starting point, will not have any luxury real estate at all. For instance, if the average price in a market is $600,000 and we adopt a three times multiple, then luxury real estate would have to be at least $1.8 million or above to qualify as luxury material.

Estimated Luxury Market Using the
2-3 x Average Price Definition

.0015%

◼ **US Housing Market: 70,000,000 homes**

◼ **Luxury Market: 100,000 homes (estimated)**

Some markets just won't have that caliber of property. This means that sometimes the most expensive home in a local market will not necessarily qualify as a luxury home. It also means that not every town in America will have luxury real estate, which is fine with me. In my view, any attempt to create a definition that allows for every town to have luxury property democratizes something that by definition is meant to be exclusive.

The starting point I am suggesting of "two to three times the average price" is meant to be an initial filter for determining if a property even qualifies. Then the expert needs to see if the property has the "requisite qualities" of a luxury property.

These subjective "requisite qualities" could include: originality, rarity, celebrity value or history. They can consist of spacious bathrooms or designer kitchens. Or, the property may have a truly outstanding address, tremendous land for the area, or breathtaking views. Perhaps it has architectural details or exquisite decorating that may be beyond what is considered normal in that market. In general, requisite qualities are attributes that set the property apart from others in more ways than just price.

Developing a Sense of Requisite Qualities

To develop a sense of "requisite qualities," I suggest looking to publications such as *Unique Homes* and *Architectural Digest*, which specialize in these types of properties. In addition, nearly all local markets have their own home and lifestyle magazines to showcase the best of local good taste. These magazines (and websites dealing with luxury real estate) can help to develop a sense of the "requisite qualities" pertinent to your specific local market.

While this book is about developing the core *power marketing* mindset and skill set that will enable you to handle luxury real estate in any market, you also must know your market's "requisite qualities" instantly. Once you do, you will be able to utilize the two to three times average price qualifier, add to it "requisite qualities," and you will know luxury real estate when you see it.

For instance, I know that in my hometown of Greenwich a $2 million or $3 million home, while beautiful, is really the average—a starter home for many in this market. Similarly, in Manhattan, $2 million to $3 million fetches a decent two- or three-bedroom apartment in a good neighborhood, but it's not going to get a spread in *Architectural Digest* any time soon (unless it's a studio). For that, you have to go over $5 million. The same is true in La Jolla, Newport Beach, Sonoma Valley, Marin County, and dozens of other luxury markets.

The Big Trophy

Armed with this new definition you are on your way to determining how big your luxury real estate market is. Have no doubt that it will be elite. In fact, it will be so small that unless you are in the largest, most liquid markets, you may wonder why you should bother.

On this point let's be clear: the luxury market represents the richest and most successful people. However tiny, it is the playing field where you want to be, where winning provides rewards far beyond each match. This is the field where everyone in the real estate market is a spectator, all watching you. This is the field on which you can earn not just enormous commissions, but also prestige, press, and glory. As a welcome by-product, understanding *power marketing* will provide skills essential for all real estate transactions and gain you market share far beyond the luxury niche.

The Takeaway

- The "million-dollar-and-up" market is less than 1 percent of the entire housing market.

- "Million-dollar-and-up" nonetheless has been superseded in many luxury markets where million-dollar sales are quite ordinary.

- The "top 10 percent" definition expands the market to almost ten times the Census and SCF average and is therefore too broad a definition.

- A better solution for defining luxury real estate is "two to three times the average price + requisite qualities," which admittedly puts luxury real estate in a rarified group.

- This definition is adaptive to individual markets, but it is also possible that some markets will have no luxury real estate.

- Focusing on the upper end of the market is the single best way to success in the whole market.

3

Five Ways (and More) Luxury Markets Are Different

Whether defined as "million dollar and up" or "two to three times the average price + requisite qualities," the luxury market is much, much smaller than most imagine. This smallness constitutes its most fundamental difference and necessitates the compelling marketing techniques I have dubbed *power marketing*. This chapter explores that smallness and other qualities that make the luxury market and luxury marketing different from the mass market.

Difference 1: Luxury Markets Are Small, Illiquid, and Sometimes Even Nonexistent

Just how small is the market that our luxury sellers are asking us to access?

In the Most Liquid Markets

Using my "two times average price + requisite qualities" definition, a study of the MLS in the most luxurious and liquid markets (Beverly Hills, Manhattan, Greenwich, the Hamptons, and Palm Beach), shows about 12 percent to 15 percent of the buyers annually seek out such homes. If we used "three times average price," it would be around 9 percent. But remember, this is true only in a handful of towns that represent the largest, most liquid markets, and that's as big as the luxury market gets.

In the National Market

There's no hard data on how many properties make up the national market using the "two to three times average price" definition, so that data awaits compiling. Based upon the much more generous "million dollar and up" definition used by the Census and SCF, we concluded in the last chapter that the luxury market constituted less than 1 percent of the seventy million owner-occupied housing units or 700,000 homes.

In reality, the yearly buyer market is about one-twentieth that number.

Why? Because all these buyers are not in the market at the same time.

In fact, at any one time about 4 to 9 percent of all homeowners are potential buyers; say an average of 5%.

> Five percent of those 700,000 million-dollar-and-up homeowners, or about 30,000 to 40,000 sales annually, constitute the million-dollar-and-up sales market.

Five percent of those 700,000 million-dollar-and-up homeowners is about 30,000 to 40,000 sales annually. Utilizing my narrower "two to three times average price + requisite qualities" definition, I estimate that my definition reduces it even further by at least a factor of five to about 6,000 to 8,000 sales annually, an extremely small number, indeed.[12]

Look at it visually to the right.

Thus, whether you use the "million dollar and up" definition and a market that is one-twentieth of less than 1 percent, or if you follow my more restrictive "two to three times average price + requisite qualities" definition, the target market is extraordinarily tiny.

Size of the US Luxury Market
Using the Three Definitions

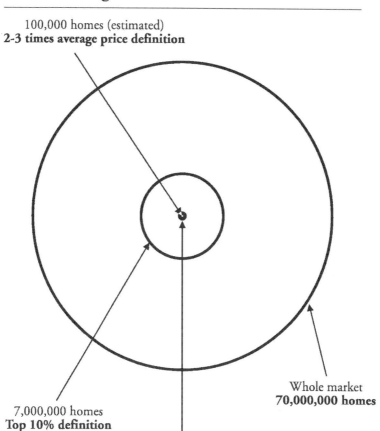

100,000 homes (estimated)
2-3 times average price definition

7,000,000 homes
Top 10% definition

<700,000 homes
<1% definition

Whole market
70,000,000 homes

Tell Our Clients

One of the biggest mistakes made by both luxury sellers and brokers is believing that the luxury market is bigger than it really is. Most luxury clients do not know this, but need to. Knowing this would help clients put into perspective how difficult it is to find luxury buyers and why agents

I estimate that my definition reduces it even further by at least a factor of five to about 6,000 to 8,000 sales annually, an extremely small number, indeed.

need to market luxury properties differently. Also, is it any wonder that sellers lacking this information are often less willing to compensate and incentivize agents accordingly?

The Mistakes It Leads To

I have witnessed countless listing presentations in which agents, trying to establish their connection to the luxury market, will boast to sellers how many multimillion-dollar buyers they have. I have also watched incredulously as agents wave their arms assuring sellers that the market is large and they will have no difficulties accessing it.

This false impression causes many problems: it leads to mistakes in pricing (often overpricing) and confusion about the expected time on market (longer), gives the impression that any agent is qualified to represent the sale, and most importantly, it obscures the need to market, reach and handle the target buyers differently from an ordinary sale. Committing any one of these mistakes can cost sellers considerably—possibly millions of dollars—and cause unneeded frustration.

Luxury homeowners have the same misimpression that the market is larger than it is, because interconnectivity among the wealthy encourages them to think their circle represents a larger part of the world than it actually does. Their social circles also tend to be fairly insular; people move to wealthy developments and restricted communities both consciously and unconsciously to be "gated" by price, people, and reputation against the realities of the rest of the market. The result is a small world that seems larger than it is.

When presenting this information to the client, do not be surprised if they respond in disbelief. However, it is better for them to know these facts up front, instead of discovering the truth only after a failed listing and marketing effort. Once buyers and sellers accept and understand the small size of the luxury market (even just the million-dollar-and-up market), then it is easier to recognize the need for *power marketing* expertise to achieve the same results that the larger market pretty much does on its own.

A Word About Liquidity

Not only are luxury markets small, but they often lack the liquidity expected from real estate markets in the United States. This, too, is due to the tendency of the rich to cloister together. Thus, moves in the luxury market—up and down—can occur with a herd instinct and with little notice. The rich seem to get richer as a group and when the tide turns they also seem to have their wealth reduced as a group.

Of course the wealthy are largely invested in the stock market, often through the same bank trust departments, mutual funds, and money managers. As a result when their wealth declines or rises, it does so en masse, giving the luxury real estate markets wild swings in liquidity. Unit sales can easily drop by 50 to 80 percent even when the overall market might be experiencing only a 10 to 20 percent drop.

During the 1990–1991 recession, my colleagues and I sat in our Park Avenue offices with paltry buyer response to a slew of different marketing efforts. Week after week our showing agents provided field reports of no showings for our listings. The few offers came from bottom feeders who provided sometimes bizarre terms (we once had an offer of twenty gallons of prized bull sperm on a $2 million house). During this recession, it was easy to think the rich had disappeared altogether.

> Moves in the luxury market—up and down—can occur with a herd instinct and with little notice. The rich seem to get richer as a group and when the tide turns they also seem to have their wealth reduced as a group.

More recently, in early 2009 I was not surprised to read in the *Stribling Luxury Residential Report* about the $5-million-and-up luxury co-op market in Manhattan. The report read, "...it is not possible to determine the price declines in this sector because there is simply not enough empirical data to suggest a pattern."[13] As a result, Stribling had to look to the market under $5M where it said, "There have been enough transactions to determine that this market has seen prices decrease 15 to 20 percent." But even in this "more liquid" market, Stribling had to give an estimated range instead of real figures. Not surprisingly, that summer Stribling found the market so slow that it suspended the luxury market report for that period altogether.[14]

Of course, we all know that wealth did not disappear in either 1990 or 2008–2009. What had disappeared en masse was the confidence of the rich. Those who still had money found themselves frozen into doing nothing until the economic outlook cleared.

Difference 2: Pricing Is More Difficult, Volatile, and Far Less Precise

Because luxury markets are thin, there is less useful data on pricing. So much about being rich is about differentiation from everyone else. Thus, by their nature, luxury homeowners go out of their way to spend considerable sums creating distinctive properties, which are more difficult to price than the average home.

Unique Products = Inexact Pricing Guesses

The mass market can more readily estimate—and even set prices—because it has a homogeneity of products and the liquidity that luxury markets lack. Luxury markets are composed of unique homes that offer fewer market comparisons upon which to draw a valuation. This makes pricing luxury homes more of an art than a science.

The reality of pricing luxury real estate is that neither the seller nor the agent really knows the price at which the property will sell. While both use experience, intuition, and empirical information—talking to neighbors, past sales—to determine price, this process is still a kind of soothsaying. There is no guarantee that any of the prior sales are going to be relevant to this sale. The seller may get much more than prior sales indicate, or, because the markets may have changed, may get less.

> Luxury markets are composed of unique homes that offer fewer market comparisons upon which to draw a valuation.

If mistakes in pricing are to be made, sellers like to see them on the high side. However, a seller who prices on the high side may have buyers dismiss the property entirely without even bothering to view it. What buyers want, after all, is a property where value is discernible and can be both articulated and defended.

In addition, using a past sales methodology of pricing can be a source of frustration for a luxury seller who thinks that "my property is better than those" and should sell for more. In fact, no matter how many comparable properties are presented to luxury homeowners, they are always likely to say nothing is comparable to theirs.

Developer's Frustration: Old Product versus New Product

Similarly, developers get frustrated by agents' past sales pricing. Because developers are often bringing to market an entirely new product, they feel that the agent, by comparing it to what has been sold in the past, is pricing it incorrectly. They reason that in markets where new products are being introduced, pricing should always be a function of what other new products are simultaneously being made available—not what has sold in the past. If there is no new product that competes with the developer's for views, luxury, space, or convenience, then the developer feels that pricing should indeed be more elastic and agents more flexible. As a result, developers are more willing to set new high price points. In many markets it is the developers, not the real estate agents, who are responsible for record prices.

Given this volatility of values, our sellers' incomparable expectations, and our developer-clients' desire for record pricing, it is clear that pricing is much more difficult and different at this end of the market, less precise, and highly volatile.

Difference 3: Sellers Do Not Have to Sell and Buyers Do Not Have to Buy. The Absence of Necessity as a Driving Force Creates a Lack of Urgency to Act on the Part of All

On the whole, this market is not characterized by the basic necessities of living; you are not dealing with basic shelter. Rather, as a *power marketer,* you are promoting a luxury item that buyers can pass on and that sellers often find no urgency to sell.

Sellers Who Do Not Have to Sell

John Maynard Keynes wrote that markets can remain irrational longer than we can remain solvent.

> One of the perks of being rich is that you have staying power to withstand market declines and can wait to get your price.

One of the perks of being rich is that you have staying power to withstand market declines and can wait to get your price. Most million-dollar-and-up sellers have more than one home and many different sources of equity. Often their homes are not leveraged but paid for in cash and thus they have no financial urgency to act. Or, if they have to raise cash, they have more liquid assets that they can sell before they entertain low-ball offers on their homes.

Buyers Who Do Not Have to Buy

In the same vein, buyers of multi-million-dollar homes do not have to buy. They can wait, too. For them, buying is more a lifestyle choice than a necessity. It does not have to happen today or tomorrow or next month. After all, the rich did not become so by being impatient; they became rich because they waited for the right opportunity to act. Wealthy buyers are not likely to move into a deal unless it is consummated on their timetable.

Buyers who do not have to buy and sellers who do not have to sell together create a lack of urgency to act. A luxury real estate broker recognizes that special tactics are needed to break this stalemate.

Difference 4: Sellers Are Highly Sophisticated, Great Negotiators, and Very Smart

Dealing with affluent clients can be a wonderful and exciting experience. But the ability to manage them (often for their own best interest) is more challenging at the luxury level than in normal real estate. How does an agent convey to the president or CEO of a Fortune 500 company that she knows more than he does about marketing his own property?

The sellers' sophistication extends to negotiating. It is likely that your clients have endured endless negotiations for the purchase of companies, other homes, boats, or artwork. They are probably adept, unafraid, and unashamed to negotiate everything. Negotiating with a buyer or seller of a $200,000 listing is not the same as with a buyer or seller of a $4 million or $20 million listing. You must have a different arsenal of *power marketing* expertise in the form of dialogues and scripts ready to call upon in luxury real estate.

Difference 5: Buyers Are Just as Smart as Sellers

In all my listing presentations, I tell my sellers that luxury buyers are just as smart as luxury sellers.

Sellers sometimes forget this and want to hire an agent who they hope can pull the wool over a buyer's eyes and get them to foolishly overpay for a property. In particular, I have found that sellers in the luxury market are most curious about international buyers, hoping that we will find a sheikh or a foreign magnate to overpay for their home. They fail to understand that buyers can afford a multimillion-dollar property, not because they got rich making silly mistakes, but because they earned their money making wise decisions. Overpaying for a home is not among them.

> Buyers can afford a multimillion-dollar property, not because they got rich making silly mistakes, but because they earned their money making wise decisions.

Remember this phrase: "In luxury real estate, buyers are just as smart as sellers." By including this phrase in your listing presentation, you are not only helping your clients understand the nature of the luxury real estate market, but you are grounding their sometimes unrealistic expectations.

Occasionally, Buyers Are Even Smarter

Sometime, the buyers of luxury property are smarter than the sellers. Why? In some cases, sellers of luxury property are worn out by the negotiating process. Oftentimes weary retirees are more eager to sell than to engage in drawn-out negotiations. Similarly, it is not uncommon to find that those with inherited wealth are less willing to bargain. Not only did they inherit the money that allowed them to buy their home, they may have inherited the home itself. Sometimes, these sellers find hard bargaining to be an intrusion into their more genteel world.

The Buyer's Advisers

Even if you find an unaware buyer, he or she almost always has a slew of lawyers, accountants, bankers, or other trusted financial advisers who ensure the buyer does not overpay for a property.

Never accept a listing assignment hoping that you will find someone uninformed enough to overpay. If, by chance, you do find that uninformed buyer, you can be sure to find a sophisticated committee of professionals put in place to prevent their client from making this mistake.

The Secondary Differences

While these five primary differences are the core of this chapter, six secondary differences also distinguish the luxury market from the mass market. Let's put them in their proper perspective and then end with surprising ways in which the luxury and mass markets are actually similar.

Secondary Difference 1: The Value of Luxury Marketing

Luxury sales enhance your prestige in ways that doing low-end sales do not. Selling a lot of low-end properties may generate income, volume and unit sales, but it will not get you multi-million-dollar listings. But selling multi-million-dollar luxury properties implies that if you can handle a prestigious sale, you can also handle any sale in the whole market. Additionally, luxury sales can increase your average price and therefore your gross commission income and volume of sales. For a firm that upholds the elite image of being successful at luxury marketing, it can attract quality agents, thereby improving the expertise of all its agents, and allowing it to better sell the whole market. But it doesn't work the same way if your niche is the low end. It is much easier to sell down from the top than to sell up from the bottom.

> It is much easier to sell down from the top than to sell up from the bottom.

Secondary Difference 2: Volume and Units Will Always Be Small

Luxury real estate cannot compete with the yardsticks of the mass market: volume and units. The number of units a luxury marketing firm sells will always be less than in the mass market. The same is often true for the volume of sales, despite the fact that luxury properties sell at higher prices. All kinds of internal debates about doing more units and volume versus enhancing image can ignite. While luxury marketing may help enhance a firm's image by providing public relations value, it is never going to win the volume and unit contest.

> While luxury marketing may help enhance a firm's image by providing public relations value, it is never going to win the volume and unit contest.

Secondary Difference 3: Luxury Marketing Costs More

Whereas the costs of selling any home includes an MLS listing fee, a sign, Internet, and other publicizing, the cost of selling a luxury property is higher. Image advertising in prestigious magazines often runs in the thousands of dollars per page and can quickly reach $10,000 or more. Open houses, photography, and brochures can also quickly rack up thousands in up-front expenses. Additionally, video imaging and stand-alone websites for individual properties consume big budgets and lots of time. There are also many ancillary costs such as quality business cards, listing and promotional material, stationery, the list goes on.

It is also important to factor in the overhead cost of your having to be present for every showing. That alone can take valuable time away from other activities and even reduce overall productivity.

Secondary Difference 4: Listing Time Is Longer

In the mass market, agents are urged to sell properties within thirty days. The mass market mandate to know out a sale a day, a week, a month doesn't hold in the luxury market. Often, this pressure to sell forces luxury agents to flee to boutique firms, which they feel better understand that agents, operating alone, cannot sell a million-dollar property each day, week, or often even within a month.

When I was working at LandVest, our minimum listing period was one year—often it was eighteen months and occasionally even two years. Sales often occurred only after eighteen months. Back then, Sotheby's would often take a twenty-four-month listing; at Previews' originally a twenty-four-month listing was largely the rule. All were ample proof that no matter what time period a firm or an agent sets, the listing agreement must be longer than the customary listing time. How much longer? Check to see how many years' supply of listings are in your luxury market (however you define it) and then use that as the minimum length of any luxury listing agreement.

If it will take an average of eighteen months to sell a property, then that is the listing time needed to protect the investment of money and time you will be making. After reading this book, you should be able to sell a luxury property in less than the average time simply because you will better understand luxury marketing. But that does not mean you should take shorter listings: luxury markets can change on a dime; you need to protect yourself against swings in the market and other unexpected events.

Secondary Difference 5: The Luxury Market Is Interconnected

Agents often note that the luxury market is different because the buyers and sellers are interconnected. The rich have preparatory school and elite college connections as well as those through the Social Register and club networks such as university or athletic clubs around the world. Similarly, the rich go to many of the same restaurants, stay at four-star resorts, and travel together on excursions and tours—often on the same cycling vacations or wine-tasting trips.

> At the luxury level there exists a transcontinental neighborliness of the wealthy.

It is not unusual to find that your buyers and sellers sit on similar boards, belong to the same clubs, or socialize together. This holds true beyond just local geography. Wealthy buyers and sellers in Washington know their counterparts in New York, Boca Raton, and Palm Beach. Dallas knows Houston. Chicago knows

Naples and Pensacola. Los Angeles knows Aspen and Vail knows New York. The intertwined nature of these markets is legendary and quite different from the mass market where neighbors might know each other but further connections become more tenuous. At the luxury level there exists a transcontinental neighborliness of the wealthy.

Indeed, it is a club that extends to luxury agents who often congregate in smaller boutique firms. Such firms mirror the elite nature of the market in which they are focused. Even at large franchises like Prudential, Coldwell Banker, and Keller Williams, the luxury agents usually form their own groups that have their own cocktail parties, networking events, and sometimes even use their own terminology.

Secondary Difference 6: The Luxury Home Is a Form of Speech for the Rich that Addresses the Non-Investment Value of Luxury Real Estate

The mass real estate market buys a place to live, a place to let the kids play, grow old and enjoy the privacy of the property around them. The same is somewhat true for the luxury market except that wealthy buyers are also making a much larger lifestyle statement.

"Defying" the Advisers to the Rich

The writers of *Wealth* treat real estate as just another investment allocation. Modern Portfolio Theory (MPT) teaches—and *Wealth* preaches—that there is value in asset allocation and diversification, and therefore real estate should be one of many investments, just not too much of the whole.

What surprises the authors of *Wealth*, including their former chief of wealth management strategies and analytics, is that "a number of HNWIs...have profited enormously by defying MPT's asset allocation provisions" by going beyond the percentage that investment advisers recommend should be invested in real estate.

The fundamental and profound question that *Wealth* raises is why luxury real estate is so highly prized as a preferred asset by HNWIs. Why do the rich prize it so much that they "defy" their advisers? If the rich are defying their advisers because they want to over-allocate to real estate, then as a real estate counselor and adviser, you need to see the opportunity lurking here.

The Non-Investment Value of a Home

By viewing luxury real estate as just another asset allocation, the investment advisory business misses the non-investment value of a luxury home. Wealth advisers overlook the indispensable role it plays in the human psyche. They miss that it is integral to psychological needs and grounded in desires, fears, and hopes. It directly relates to primal aspects of the human psyche and human condition.[15]

> No one gives guests a tour of their investment portfolio.

Luxury property is one of the single most important socially defining purchases that wealthy individuals make. It is how wealth is displayed and enjoyed in America. No one gives guests a tour of their investment portfolio. A luxury home allows the rich to distinguish themselves from the merely affluent. That is why HNWIs ignore their advisers and spend more on homes.

To be successful *power marketers*, like the auctioneer in Chapter 1, you need to know that there is this large emotional and psychological component to the desire for luxury real estate.

The non-investment value of luxury real estate has yet another aspect: our luxury clients engage in a kind of language among themselves. They "talk" through the idiom of the real estate they buy. Luxury property acts like a billboard advertising to the world who they are, what they have accomplished, how much money they have and how old their money is.

Sometimes they want to convey privacy and they buy homes in remote areas. Sometimes they want great street presence or they make their statement with high walls and big gates from the curbside. While every home is a reflection of the personality of its purchaser, at the luxury end that notion is taken to a radical degree.

These, then, are the five primary differences and six secondary differences of marketing luxury real estate versus mass market real estate. Let's now conclude with a few similarities between the two that we should be certain not to ignore.

Similarities to Mass Marketing

I can relate to the disdain luxury agents can have for mass market techniques. I, too, have attended seminars where wonderful coaches and trainers tell agents to cold call prospects, canvass a neighborhood, or set out door hangers. I have been coached on buying the refrigerator calendars and about taking clients to the kitchen table because "that is where all important decisions are made."

Once, when I was a new and naïve aspiring luxury agent, I tried to take a lovely dowager who was a potential client to her kitchen table. When I asked her which way it might be, she, who had a butler, two maids, a cook, and a waiter, smiled incredulously at me and said, "I have no idea. I have never been."

The advice that is given to real estate agents on a general spectrum does not always translate well to the luxury market. Nonetheless, as a luxury agent you cannot dwell only on the preceding differences, but need to understand some of the important sales similarities.

Similarity 1: Luxury Marketing Is About Selling, Not Club Membership

As a luxury agent you are in the sales business, just like all real estate agents. You are a salesperson, not a member of a private club. If you have convinced yourself that the "sales stuff" is beneath you, then you may be neglecting the very techniques that could, in fact, make you more successful. If you focus too much on how different you are and fail daily to practice prospecting and lead generation techniques (something most agents dislike), you hurt your own business and you won't make it in any market, mass or luxury.

You are in sales, not snobbery. Your personal goal should be to list, sell, and earn a commission like every other agent. Many luxury clients, both buyers and sellers, are likely to have some kind of sales or business background, and they are probably also very good at it. They, above all others, are positioned to recognize and appreciate a good salesperson—and will pay generously to hire an excellent one.

Do not be afraid to think of yourself as a salesperson. A super salesperson requires an understanding of sales psychology few jobs require. When you are trying to list a luxury property—say, that of a CEO—know that when you talk sales to them, you are speaking their language.

> **If you have convinced yourself that the "sales stuff" is beneath you, then you may be neglecting the very techniques that could, in fact, make you more successful**

Similarity 2: Need for Hard Data

Because the luxury end of the market is sometimes thin on data and because accessing it can be more difficult than in the mass market, some agents will give up and rely on gut or whim.

Don't do it. You cannot operate at the luxury end on gut feel or on a whim. You cannot say that a property is "so unique" that no comparative data exist. There is always data because even the lack thereof is data, Isn't it?

If, for instance, there is a lack of comparable sales, that is a risk of marketing a particular luxury property. And if you proceed, you must share the lack of comparables with your sellers. Everyone must know in advance that they are navigating uncertain terrain.

But there is always data that can help put the luxury market into some perspective. Just keeping a list of all luxury sales over a certain price point, for example, provides an excellent perspective on the market. It often allows the seller to see the small number of sales versus the overall market, and the price points for such sales. In many cases it can provide the actual selling price of a property rumored to have sold for something higher. The need for correct information in luxury marketing is no less than in the mass-market arena, and the difficulty in acquiring it is no excuse for proceeding without the facts.

Similarity 3: CMAs and BPOs for Pricing

Luxury real estate agents have to do a Comparative Market Analysis (CMA) and a Broker Price Opinion (BPO), just like other agents. That includes looking at past sales and those currently available, separating out the improvements from the land, pricing them individually, and doing a replacement value analysis to price a house. Agents have to do this no matter how exceptional the home. Similarly, for apartments in urban areas, agents have to see how prices compare per square foot for a luxury apartment to the overall market and to the highest prices paid. They also have to consider what something costs new versus used.

Although pricing luxury real estate is tougher than mass market pricing, it is still possible and it must be done. CMAs and BPOs for luxury real estate are always possible, and are, in fact, even more essential to defending value to the sophisticated buyers with whom you will be negotiating.

> Because the luxury market is so small, with so many agents trying to get into it, leads are harder to come by and we must allocate more time to prospecting and generating leads, not less.

Similarity 4: Leads, Leads, and more Leads

Luxury real estate agents must generate leads to stay in business. Often when I ask luxury agents how they get their leads, they shrug it off as simply "knowing so many people." While this may be the case for a very select few, most often this answer is code for avoiding lead generation. Successful luxury agents devote most of their time to generating leads. This means asking for referrals, partnering with a retiring agent, spending a significant portion of your time making contacts and spreading word of your credentials. All this is more important in the luxury market than in the mass market because there are fewer leads to be had.

> **Successful luxury agents devote most of their time to generating leads. This means asking for referrals, partnering with a retiring agent, spending a significant portion of your time making contacts and spreading word of your credentials**

Similarity 5: Scripts, Role Playing, Objection Handling

As a luxury agent you need to master scripts and engage in script practice, role playing, and objection handling, just like any good salesperson. Because of the sophistication of your clientele, this is no place for you to "wing it" rather than have mastered ready-to-use scripts. The need to be scripted and composed is so much greater than in the mass market. Your luxury client can easily spot an amateur. And remember, luxury clients expect more, and are willing to pay more for better skill.

At stake is not a $6,000 commission, but a $200,000 or a $400,000 commission. This requires the professional ability to deliver scripts flawlessly and handle objections with ease.

Similarity 6: Focus and Specialization

Finally, just as in the mass market, your luxury business grows by narrowing your focus to one town, one neighborhood, one complex of condominiums and then staying clearly focused on demonstrating your expertise and knowledge of the upper end within that geographic area. There are no more powerful words you can say to a seller in a listing presentation than, "I specialize in what you own." When a seller hears you say, "I only focus on the upper end of the market and I only represent sellers," you have provided a compelling connection to them and an equally compelling reason for them to hire you. Your focus and specialization sets you apart. You have positioned yourself to offer exactly what they need. Specialize and stay focused on listing properties within the luxury end of a specified market and you will own the advantage every highly specialized agent enjoys versus the generalist.

The Takeaway _____

🎩 The luxury market is different for five primary reasons.

- It is much smaller and very thinly traded, creating illiquidity.
- Pricing is more difficult.
- Sellers do not have to sell and buyers do not have to buy, creating a lack of urgency to act.
- Sellers are more sophisticated than in the mass market.
- Buyers are just as sophisticated and smart as sellers.

🎩 These primary reasons create some secondary but important other differences.

- Luxury marketing enhances your image and that of your firm, which helps your firm score better on the mass market yardsticks of volume, units, gross commission income, etc.
- The volume of luxury unit sales will always be small.
- Marketing expenses are higher for luxury real estate.
- Sales times are longer and therefore listing agreements need to be, too.
- The rich have greater interconnectivity beyond the local marketplace.
- Luxury real estate has a primal non-investment value that can lead buyers to spend willingly and gladly.

🎩 There are important personal habits for success that all top agents, luxury and mass market, share.

- Luxury marketing is sales, not club membership.
- You always need to compile hard data or present the lack thereof.
- Present your market knowledge through professionalism and thorough CMAs and BPOs.
- Prospecting at the luxury end is just as necessary, if not more so, as in the mass market because the luxury market is smaller with more agents targeting it.

- Because of the sophistication of your clientele, you'll need to use scripts, role playing, and objection handling, just as in the mass market.

- Success comes from focus and specializing in your subject matter.

- "I only work with sellers and I specialize in what you own" are powerful words, if you are willing to add them to your listing presentation.

4

A Power Marketing Mindset

Having identified the differences between the luxury and the mass market, in this chapter you will learn about the *power marketing* mindset needed to win.

Power Marketing Mindset #1: The Smallness and Lack of Liquidity in the Luxury Markets Require that You Create a Market for Your Listings by Always Finding Two or More Buyers

Many years ago a luxury marketing firm took as its slogan, "To find that one buyer in a million." I always liked that slogan. It set the firm apart by projecting a certain exclusivity.

That said, what would happen when you as a luxury marketer find one buyer in a million? Would one buyer bid up for a property? Or would she prefer to use her "one in a million" status to negotiate a lower price because she was the only bidder?

One buyer does not a market make. A single buyer, in fact, puts the client-seller in a weaker position than before. Power shifts from the seller to the buyer, giving the latter total control. The buyer dictates the psychology, the negotiations, the terms, and ultimately the price paid for the sale.

If, as an agent, you find only one buyer, you empower him, and you put your client at a distinct disadvantage. Finding "one buyer in a million" is the opposite of *power marketing*.

Only by introducing competition can you compel the sales process toward a successful conclusion, for all parties involved.

As a *power marketer,* the competition you create deprives any one buyer control of the process. The more buyers, the greater the competition and the more power in your marketing. Without this competition, buyers will do exactly what any self-interested person would do: bid low, if at all. Due to the small scale and lack of liquidity in the luxury market, finding two or more buyers is markedly more difficult, but also imperative. Your mindset must always be focused on doing just that.

> One buyer does not a market make. A single buyer, in fact, puts the client-seller in a weaker position than before.

Step 1 is inform sellers of the small size of the luxury market, and the difficulties involved in marketing a luxury property. The very beginning of each listing presentation must include this discussion; clients must know that a large part of your job is not to put there property on the market, but to *create* the market .

In Chapter 2, I provided some statistics on how small the luxury market is, and in Chapter 3 I gave a visual of the luxury market to help you get started. Use them. They can be downloaded from my website http://PowerMarketing.pro under "Free Stuff." Supplement them with similar charts and graphs about how small your local luxury market is.

Now let's amend *Power Marketing* Mindset #1: *Power marketing requires a minimum of two buyers, or at least the perception or the threat thereof.* Let me explain what I mean by that.

There are times when you may not actually need two buyers. Rather, the perception or threat alone will suffice to create the competition central to *power marketing.*

Your Reputation for Success Can Be a Threat

As an example, a good real estate agent is a powerful threat to buyers. Why? Because knowing that the property is likely to be sold can prompt hesitant buyers to make an offer. In talking with potential buyers, I always mention my 93 percent track record of success, while expressing my confidence that the property in question—like other properties I have represented—will be sold, too.

This knowledge can even prompt a lone bidder to bid higher. Often, simply the threat of unleashing a *power marketer's* skill is enough to move a buyer to bid again, or bid more.

If a seller warns a buyer that her property is being listed with a highly successful luxury agent, the seller is harnessing the power of threat to motivate hesitant buyers, even though there are no real buyers—yet.

Why the First Offer Is Often the Best

Another example is first offers, which everyone in real estate knows are sometimes the best offer a seller gets. The reason is the threat of the unknown. This threat is only present for the first few days of a listing, when the buyer is pained by the insecurity of not yet knowing the results of a luxury agent's marketing efforts. The threat of losing the property can move first buyers to bid fast and bid high and sometimes make the seller's best offer.

Thus, while finding two or more buyers is always our mindset, it may not always be necessary. Rather, the threat of finding two or more buyers can itself provide the competition needed to prompt a successful bid (you will see this illustrated with Clarendon Court in Chapter 8).

Markets and Creating Them

Two final notes on Power Marketing Mindset #1: Over the last one hundred years, the National Association of Realtors (and its hundreds of state and local boards) have created Multiple Listing Services (MLS) in virtually every market in America. These MLSs have created what are called "universal offers of cooperation and compensation" between and among agents under which fees are shared.

As a result, the organized real estate brokerage profession has done a superb job of creating markets for most real estate. These markets are taken for granted as being liquid and efficient. They provide quality guidance on what properties have sold for in the past, and therefore what they might sell for in the future. The result is a marketplace that is transparent, accessible, efficient, and highly cost effective.

Because of the efficiency that exists in the U.S. market, most of us rarely concern ourselves with creating competitive markets for our

> Because of the efficiency that exists in the U.S. market, most of us rarely concern ourselves with creating competitive markets for our listings. Usually the markets are created for us.

listings. Usually the markets are created for us. We don't think of it as our job, let alone our goal.

But in luxury marketing our mindset must focus on *creating* a market. Lack of doing so has often prompted sellers of unsold homes to accuse their agent of never doing anything more than just "putting the property on the MLS" and holding a couple of open houses. Ironically, in most instances, the homeowner was correct that is all that their agent did because their agent thought that doing this is enough to get the job done. But for the unique and most expensive properties, there simply is no readily accessible marketplace, and while giving the property thorough exposure through the MLS is one of the most important tools available to finding buyers, *power marketing* dictates we stay focused on *creating* competition between those buyers in order to *create* a true market. It is what we do with the buyers found through the MLS that constitutes *power marketing.*

A good *power marketer* loves nothing more than the challenge of selling a magnificent property for which there is no readily discernible and accessible market. Illiquid, thin, and sometimes nonexistent markets present the ultimate challenge. *Creating* markets that hardly exist is real marketing and requires serious *power marketing* skill.

Pricing Provides Competitive Power, Too

For years, great real estate coaches and trainers have advised their agent-customers that the most effective way to sell real estate is to price properties close to or even below market value. This, they correctly argue, is how to release competition and create a market for a property.

I agree that in the mass market it is important for most agents to list only properties for which there is a market and to list them within the boundaries of price indicated by that market. Similarly, it is critical for good agents to turn down listings that are above the market.

Based on this advice, if you really want to *power market* a listing, just list it cheaply enough under the market and you will unleash a torrent of competitive demand. It will sell, and sometimes with the right *power marketing* orchestration, will even sell above the asking price. Why? Bargains unleash the competition inherent in *power marketing*. In fact, I will teach you how to create credible and defensible value that you can discount from to create a compelling bargain for buyers. Smart sophisticated buyers want value articulated and defended and if you can demonstrate a bargain, even better. Thus, when such trainers and coaches teach below market pricing to generate competitive sales, they are, in effect, teaching *power marketing*.

We Don't Have the Privilege of Low Pricing

The difference is that in the luxury market, it is simply not possible most of the time to list properties within or even below the market. Our sophisticated sellers want their incomparable properties listed above the market and they want their pricing to be as different as they perceive their properties to be.

> Our sellers want their properties listed above the market and they want their pricing to be as different as they perceive their properties to be.

Therefore, you must be able to get *power marketing* results through other means than simply pricing properties cheaply. This includes more oblique and sometimes more subtle ways to establish great value and unleash competition. I will show you how in Chapter 5, with examples in Chapters 7 and 8.

Power Marketing Mindset #2: Power Marketers Never Fix Value but Set Expectations Within Bands of Likely Value

The price a seller gets will vary with the quality of the marketing choosen. As a power marketer you must never tell your clients that their property is going to sell at a certain price. You are not being square with them, no matter how sure you may be.

At the start of a listing you must make your client sensitive to the bands of value within which expectations should be kept, and aware of the variables that will affect the outcome. These include the fact that while tradition in real estate markets calls for a fixed asking price, the selling price is not fixed and can (and will) go up or down depending on:

- Market conditions
- The number of buyers you find or the threat you can create
- The value to the buyer that you have articulated
- The cooperation of the seller
- The comfort level of the buyers
- How well you have orchestrated the psychology of the sale

Sellers intuitively know the top end of these valuation bands. When a listing agent comes into a living room with a lengthy and well researched CMA and then renders a broker price opinion (BPO) at, say, $3.7M, the seller will sometime say, "I want $4.1M instead." Why? Because sellers, perhaps more often than agents, recognize that markets

> Price expectations have to follow the changing tide.

change and are not fixed and therefore they want to "protect" themselves in the event of price spikes by going a little higher. Sellers often use the listing agent's research into past sales to educate themselves about what a reasonable price should be for their property and then just add a little more, often justifying it with "needing a little negotiating room."

> You don't control prices, you control the marketing that sets prices.

You may have felt frustrated by this tactic because often you have already included "a little extra" into your BPO. When the seller pads the price as well, this either prices the property out of the market or sets it indefensibly high, discouraging buyers and other agents. The result can be a listing that is dead before even entering the market.

Because markets are dynamic and change constantly, your mindset must be to confine selling expectations to reasonable bands of valuation—not to a fixed asking price. A property valued on April 1 may face entirely new market conditions by the time a buyer makes an offer. It is possible that by June 1, the stock market has crashed (or spiked), a war may have started, or some other event may materially affect the markets. While no one can predict the future, you know that price expectations have to follow the changing tide and your client should know it, too.

While your job is to determine a valuation range and suggest an asking price that is credible and defensible, still, it will be nothing more than a well thought out educated guess. Never tell a seller that you will get a particular fixed price. You don't control prices. You control the marketing that sets prices. With *Power Marketing* Mindset #2 you recognize the non-fixed, highly fluid nature of prices and therefore always talk about them with clients in terms of valuation bands.[16]

Power Marketing Mindset #3: Power Marketers Orchestrate Multiple Bidders, or the Threat Thereof, to Act Simultaneously

In normal markets, buyers buy because they need shelter or they want to move up socioeconomically, or are relocating, or for any number of other reasons. Buyers actually get weary of looking and want to bring the process to a close. But in the luxury market, viewing million-dollar homes and the luxury lifestyle associated with them can be fun. It can even become a hobby for luxury buyers who have time on their hands. Additionally, because our sellers do not have to sell and our buyers do not have to buy, we must overcome the market's lack of urgency to act.

The only solution is simultaneous bidding, or the threat thereof. Recall the auction: it is the presnce of many buyers filling the room (even if most will not bid the object being sold) and the awareness of each other at the same time that prompts action. It is not enough to have one buyer in March and another in May (although in the story about *Le Domaine Resistance* I will show you how to use their spacing to advantage). Rather, you must orchestrate several simultaneously. Only by reaching this moment in time will your sellers get the highest price possible for their property.

Thus, the goal of all luxury real estate marketing is to reach a point in time of having two or more buyers, or the threat thereof, bidding on a property *simultaneously.* The momentum generated from simultaneous bidding is so enticing and contagious that buyers who might be hesitant to act are swept up in the enthusiasm of the sale.

Power Marketing Mindset #4: Your Ability to Create Power Marketing Competition Raises the Comfort Level of Highly Sophisticated Sellers to Hire You

When your mindset is focused on how to place a property into a competitive situation, the sophistication of luxury sellers is met by your brokerage expertise. Then, they will hire you.

By honing your *power marketing* skills to create competition, you will speak the language of sophisticated owners. You will also personally acquire the confidence to deal with celebrities, ex-presidents, entrepreneurs, professional athletes, CEOs, and other high-powered sellers. And, just as they hire expensive caterers to prepare fancy dinner parties and hire top notch financial advisers for portfolio planning, the wealthy are more than willing to hire competent people (and pay them well) to get the job done. You just have to demonstrate the *power marketing* mindset of orchestrating multiple buyers or the threat thereof to bid simultaneously. Highly sophisticated sellers will connect with that mindset and hence with you.

> I love the phrase "Quality is remembered long after price is forgotten."

One of the benefits of working in the luxury real estate market is dealing with people who recognize quality when they see it. I love the phrase "Quality is remembered long after price is forgotten" because it is so true. The problem for the rich is not the ability or the willingness to pay; rather, it is finding competent people to hire. Once they do, they will pay handsomely and willingly.

Don't be afraid of their sophistication and success. Just master the *power marketing* mindset in this book of unleashing competition, and then tell your clients what you know; work hard at creating that competition; and be prepared to document your success for your future clients. The rest will take care of itself.

Power Marketing Mindset #5: Competition Allows Smart Buyers to Pay More

If buyers are just as smart as sellers and everyone lacks an urgency to act, then what is the mindset that gets wealthy buyers to buy? After all, if they are so smart, don't they always want a bargain? If so, then isn't the luxury market destined to have limited upside price growth because buyers are smart enough never to overpay?

Anyone going to art auctions or recalling the fictional auction I created in Chapter 1, knows that every day somewhere in the world there is a luxury auction taking place where smart, sophisticated buyers routinely pay up for objects. There we can see rich, smart people compete to pay more than other rich, smart people and sometimes set record prices. The same is true in the luxury real estate market.

> It is the presence of other buyers that gets smart buyers to pay more.

Smart buyers not only will pay up for a luxury property but will do so willingly and gladly, but only when presented with competition from their peers. *Power Marketing* begins with acknowledging how smart our buyers are. It acknowledges that our buyers can pay any amount for a property, and we would never expect them to pay more for something, unless they have to. Our job as power marketers is to find, create and then orchestrate competition so those buyers have to bid up. Thus, it is the presence of other smart buyers that gets luxury bidders to pay more or to start bidding at all.

Power Marketing Mindset #5 requires you to maintain two buyer emotions—fear of loss and buyer comfort—throughout the buying process.

Fear of Loss

Fear of loss can exist only if buyers are aware of each other, either by seeing others coming and going at showings or by telling them about other interest. Some listing agents worry about creating an "auction situation" and they keep information about multiple interest from other buyers. Doing so hurts sellers because it prevents a critical fear and important comfort from entering the negotiations. But it also offends buyers. In fact, it is not so much the presence of other bidders that causes buyers anger or pain; rather, it is not knowing of the presence of other buyers.

In my thirty years managing real estate offices the greatest number of buyer complaints have come from angry buyers who lost a property because they were never informed that other bidders were in play. They felt cheated by not having the opportunity to bid higher. Either the listing agent or the selling agent or both feared creating an "auction situation" when in fact, they should have been aiming to create one.

Your *power marketing* mindset is to control the psychology of the sale by always unleashing the fear of losing the property into the sales process. It is your job to keep the fear of loss ever-present. Only with the knowledge of other buyers bidding (or the threat thereof) on a property can emotional bidding wars begin where all justification of value is left aside. Ego might even take over the buyer, who may actually bid simply so as not to be out-bid.

During the first listing appointment, inform sellers that by controlling the psychology of the sale and getting them to the enviable point of multiple buyers bidding simultaneously, magic can happen. Tell them of the situations in which you have succeeded in creating this magic and how it worked out.

Buyer Comfort

What is ironic is that many agents discourage competition, fearing It will annoy or offend buyers, when in fact, if a sale is properly orchestrated, it does the exact opposite; it raises the comfort level of buyers to act. It is the very presence of other buyers bidding simultaneously or the threat thereof that makes intelligent buyers comfortable enough to bid higher for a property. That is why we must insure all buyers know of the presence of other buyers. Competition is what moves buyers and unleashes their willingness to pay. Just as an example, everyone in real estate knows that a buyer can be dormant for months, but suddenly when a second buyer comes along and makes an offer, the first buyer scrambles into action. In this and in so many other situations, competition prompts action. Each buyer confirms the other's good taste in location, style, and amenities. Competition increases comfort level to bid because it is what validates and confirms the wisdom of bidding at all. It is what gives buyers the assurance that if they bid just a little bit more, there is someone below them who wants this property. The greater the number of buyers, the more the assurance that they are smart to bid on this property.

Sole Buyer Syndrome Revisited

In fact, let's revisit "sole buyer syndrome." Remember that? It occurs when someone is the only buyer for a property. By not making buyers aware of other competitive interest, we risk unleashing sole buyer syndrome. In other words, that wonderful fear of losing the property which we want to maintain, can, if we don't make buyers aware of each other, morph into a different fear—the fear that they might actually get a property that no one else wants. If no one is out there validating the wisdom of the buyer's interest, the fear of loss could quickly turn into fear of gain.

And we don't want that. We want the fear of loss to be ever present.

This is the classic buyer's remorse; after obtaining the property, buyers ask themselves why they bid up for it if no one else came to the table. They begin second-guessing their actions. This almost never happens if there is another buyer on their tail.

Because buyers are just as smart as sellers, you must formulate your whole marketing strategy to appeal to it. Concede the fact that they will not willingly bid up for a property without competition. That willingness appears only when a second or third buyer surfaces and bids simultaneously. The addition of these new interested parties simultaneously creates a fear of loss that is, in turn, mitigated and overcome by the comfort of others' validation.

> Present them their competition so that they can feel both the tension of competition and the comfort of knowing others want what they want.

We therefore create the competition so that buyers can intelligently, comfortably, and gladly bid up. Together these two emotions, fear of loss and comfort in not being alone, position the buyer to bid aggressively, sometimes joyfully and usually eagerly, perhaps even exceeding the asking price.

Power Marketing Mindset #5 requires that you as a *power marketer* do not begin with trying to pull the wool over buyers' eyes nor assume that buyers are foolishly going to overpay for a property. Rather, you assume the buyers are smart, really smart. You assume that buyers are just as smart as the sellers. You want to appeal to the buyers' innate intelligence. So you take it as your task to present them their competition so that they can feel both the tension of competition and the comfort of knowing others want what they want. By presenting them their competition and validating their own wisdom In bidding, you actually liberate them of the fear of buying. You create the urgency to act. You give them the freedom to bid aggressively and not feel silly or foolish. You create the very conditions under which they can intelligently bid eagerly, if not joyfully, and if they win, feel good about their purchase.

Summary

In this chapter, I have explained that luxury markets are exceedingly small, illiquid, and sometimes even nonexistent. Because of this fact, we need to adopt a *power marketing* mindset that tries to create markets for our listings by finding two or more buyers simultaneously, or the threat thereof. Because pricing luxury real estate is difficult, imprecise, and volatile, it is important to adopt a mindset of pricing bands, which hem in expectations with reality. Your *power marketing* mindset understands that the price that the client receives is not determined by someone's valuation, but by the quality of the marketing you deliver.

Because sellers and buyers in the luxury market are highly sophisticated and demand an elite level of performance, it is your job to demonstrate the need for competitive *power marketing* and your competence at delivering it. In doing so, you rise to the level of expertise to which your clients are accustomed and for which they are prepared to pay.

A *power marketing* mindset consists of controlling and orchestrating all aspects of the psychology of the sale so that a buyer's comfort level rises to the point of overcoming the lack of urgency to act. Nothing raises their comfort level to act more than multiple buyers bidding simultaneously. When you create this situation, you actually appeal to the intelligence of buyers, acknowledging that they should bid up only when necessary.

Finally, *power marketing* competition overcomes the difficulties inherent in pricing luxury real estate by creating individual markets that ultimately determine the price a seller will receive from buyers who, when professionally prompted to do so, can provide the highest price willingly and even enthusiastically.

The Takeaway _____

🎩 *Power Marketing* **Mindset #1:** The smallness and lack of liquidity of the luxury markets requires you to find two or more buyers or at least the threat or perception thereof.

🎩 *Power Marketing* **Mindset #2:** Valuation requires setting expectations within elastic bands of value understanding that the price a seller gets will vary with the quality of the marketing chosen. Markets set prices and *power marketing* gets the highest price or the quickest sale.

🎩 *Power Marketing* **Mindset #3:** To overcome the lack of urgency to act created by a market where sellers do not have to sell and buyers do not have to buy, power marketers orchestrate multiple bidders to act simultaneously, as discussed in *Power Marketing* Mindset #1.

🎩 *Power Marketing* **Mindset #4:** Because luxury sellers are more sophisticated you must raise their comfort level to list with you by demonstrating equally sophisticated *power marketing* expertise.

🎩 *Power Marketing* **Mindset #5:** By creating competition through multiple buyers bidding simultaneously, *power marketing* acknowledges that buyers are just as smart as sellers and raises their comfort level to bid gladly.

5

Seven Step Pricing—No Fingers in the Air

E arlier I mentioned that there is always data available to price a luxury property, even if it's not comparable sales information. Let's now turn to learning about that data to determine a luxury property's core value and a credible and defensible asking price. I will also show you how to create extra value for your clients and get them thousands, and possibly hundreds of thousands of extra dollars, through just one *power marketing* technique, just as the hypothetical auctioneer in Chapter 1 was able to get $2 million more in the last minute of the auction.

On the issue of pricing you may now be asking some questions.

• How do I determine the parameters or bands within which a property might sell?

• What influences these parameters?

• Where within that valuation band should the property be listed?

• How do I arrive at a definitive asking price to put into the MLS?

• How do I make the buyer comfortable with my pricing and still have an asking price that satisfies my sellers?

• If pricing is influenced by motivation, how do I ascertain my seller's motivation?

When I first started in the luxury real estate business, my insightful senior partner, Bob Borden, usually accompanied me on listing appointments. Invariably, early in the meeting, the seller would ask, "So what price do you think you can get?" or, "What do you think it is worth?"

We never had any idea what price the seller would get because we had not yet begun to ask enough questions. Even by the time Bob and I left the living room, we often still did not know. Pricing was always something that was just too important simply to stick our fingers in the air and pull out a price.

Pricing is a matter of determining risk levels—both yours and those of your seller. Pricing is something agents stake reputations on. Accurate pricing forms the core of the financial bet you and your company make on a listing and on which you spend a lot of marketing money. For everyone involved it represents a huge time commitment.

Therefore, it is an investment in which you are trying to gauge the risk and the probability of reward on your money and time. Luxury real estate marketing, like all businesses, has to generate returns; each listing should be subjected to a serious risk-reward analysis. You must ask, "At what price can I sell this property and can I make any money doing so?"

For Bob and me, pricing was something that we would talk about sometimes for days. Often these conversations occurred at our weekly sales meetings, where we would present our data before the sales force and get reactions. Always we were gauging our and our client's risk against the rewards. Even if the seller knew what price he wanted, we still utilized the same routine, the same exercise you will find here, each and every time.

Today I'd posit that pricing luxury real estate cannot be determined by a computer or a website because every luxury property is different. Good pricing requires experience and judgment in weighing the many variables and even then it is only an educated guess.

> Good pricing requires experience and judgment in weighing the many variables and even then it is only an educated guess.

Part of the purpose of this book is to help you acquire the judgment to assess those variables and come up with a credible and defensible asking price. As you know, that price has to satisfy a seller who does not want to leave any money on the table. Yet, the price must be defensible to agents and the buyers they represent. As an agent you are challenged with pricing something that has few comparables, little data, and tremendous subjectivity.

Here are the seven steps to getting it done.

Step 1. Establish a Core Value Range

Begin by analyzing a luxury property's core or intrinsic value, much as a securities analyst will examine book value as the bedrock value for a security. Security analysts know that over time all securities trade above and below book value. Book value, therefore, has nothing to do with market value or the asking price or with the price you get for it. But it is a start for creating and anchoring a pricing reference point.

The analogy to book value would seem to one drawback: valuing property can result in broad variations, but book value is a clearly defined number on a company's balance sheet, right? Wrong—behind that number are dozens, sometimes hundreds of assumptions made by management and their accountants, often buried in the footnotes and small print. As a result, accountants have created Byzantine rules for trying to render all valuations based upon common determinations, but in the end, it is the assumptions management makes about the value of assets and liabilities on the company's books that can render similarly broad variations in a company's book value.

In real estate, we have just as many assumptions that go into determining the core value of a property and just as much subjectivity. Don't be afraid of that fact. It is part of valuing anything. What is important is that we have thought through all the assumptions and disclosed them, not that we made them. The core value will always be subject to interpretation, just like book value, and will be a range based upon the assumptions made about all the components of a property.

When in a living room with my sellers, I like to walk them through how to determine the core or book value of their homes. I warn them that this is not an exercise to determine the asking price but rather an evaluation of the components of the property plus a few assumptions and subjective adjustments.

Sometimes this exercise alarms sellers who just want to know what price I will get for them. Others only want to know if I can get them their desired price. Sometimes, because of the sensitivity of walking them through the various components that make up the value of their

> The core value will always be subject to interpretation, just like book value, and will be a range based upon the assumptions made.

property, we cannot do this exercise at all—or at least not with them present. This could also mean that the seller is not motivated to list the property, or that there may be other issues that need to be uncovered. But rest assured that many buyers (and some agents) are going to engage in a similar exercise within minutes of viewing the property. Our job is to have done it first and then persuade them that our assumptions are the correct ones.

The formula for core value is:

Range of Land + Range of Replacement Cost Reduced by Obsolescence and Age + Range of Amenities = Range of Core (Book) Value

The Land Value

Whenever I view a property, the first thing I ask is: What is the land worth without the house and improvements? What would a vacant piece of land in this location with this terrain and these views be worth? If it is a two-acre lot, what are these lots going for? If it is four acres, what is that number? If it is waterfront, what is the going rate per front foot? Adjust all values for views, hills, wetlands, streams, rocky soil, sewer and water, access, etc. In the end, determine a high-low range for the underlying basic land value.

If, by chance, there is no past sale, say for seven acres of waterfront, because none has been available for twenty years, that is still important to know and note. There is a scarcity value here (more about that later). In this instance, find the last land sales, adjust them for inflation, or even better, if you know the historical appreciation rates in that area, adjust the sales using those rates. Alternatively, find other current sales where properties may have been bought and torn down and try to infer a value. But get a range of value for just the land.

Add the Replacement Value for Improvements

Second, determine what it costs to build a luxury house per square foot in this market. To find out, all you have to do is ask three builders. Pick three separate builders who specialize in affordable, middle market, and luxury housing. You will then get the whole range of building costs in your market. Or talk with two to three homeowners who recently built a house. They know the likely range. Every real estate agent should know these costs at all times. Take the range of costs per square foot to build it new and multiply the square footage times that building cost.

Adjust the Replacement Cost for Age

Depending on the local relative demand in the market for new or old, I generally give a home a forty-year life. If it costs $2M to replace the home and it is ten years old, I take the $2M replacement cost, divide by forty years, and get a yearly deduction for age and obsolescence. Multiply that yearly deduction by the age of the home. In this example, reduce for 10 years ($2M divided by 40 years = $50,000 a year × 10 years of age = a reduction from replacement cost of $500,000). This nets a value adjusted for obsolescence of $1.5M ($2M less $500,000 for obsolescence). You certainly do not have to accept my forty-year figure. You can use any assumption you wish that you believe is appropriate for your market.

Unfortunately, this does not work well for an antique home or for a home that has been meticulously maintained. If a home is in perfect condition, you may have to value it at the same price as new. It also does not work well for homes with spectacular detail that would cost a fortune to replace (a castle or a palace, for example). Do not value such details at the replacement cost because fine craftsmanship also incurs high maintenance costs. But for most luxury properties, the above formula works.

Step 2. Adjust for Factors that Add Value and Others that Limit Value to Get the Adjusted Core Value Range

Once you arrive at a core value range, you now have to adjust the core value for other factors. The land can be adjusted up or down for:

UPWARD FACTORS	DOWNWARD FACTORS
Abuts conservation land	Near highway
Superior privacy	Near another home
Flat, nice lot	Wetlands on or near property
Hilly lot	Noise
	Clearly inferior neighbors
	No record of any area sales

Similarly, the house can be adjusted up or down for:

UPWARD FACTORS	DOWNWARD FACTORS
Slate roof	Eight maid's rooms
Superior finishes	No air conditioning
Least expensive house in area	Most expensive house in area
Views	Design flaws
Beauty	Dated
Celebrity value	

Each market is different. A positive factor in one market can be a negative in another. There are hundreds of variables for which you must adjust up or down. Like the amenities discussion below, it is useful to conduct this exercise at an office meeting to help everyone gain the experience of evaluating local trends and understanding appropriate pricing adjustments. The more contributors to this discussion, the better. But *power marketers* in any luxury market should know these factors stone cold and be able to discuss them with every seller.

Add the Amenity Value

Amenities include a septic system, pool, waterfall, driveways, fencing, landscaping, outdoor spas, tennis court, outdoor lighting, retaining walls, etc. First, make a list of what your local market views as amenities and then put a ballpark price on them (this is an ideal office meeting exercise). Again, the contractors in the market should be able to estimate these or give you a likely range. Every real estate office should build a list of the providers of amenities and should update these cost figures once a year.

Amenities can sometimes include things like a septic system. What does it cost to install a new one? If it has a pool, what does that cost today? Landscaping? Tennis court? Spa? Landscaping is an exception because it can be valued above replacement cost since it can actually increase in value over time as mature landscaping can have greater value than new. I would not fuss too much on exactitude. Rather, make clear what your value is. Your seller

> Core value is often a high figure that can be discounted to represent the bargain our highly value-conscious buyers always insist on buying.

may disagree with it and can then put in a different value, but always the operative question is: How much would someone value this amenity today in its present condition? Calculate all these costs

The Convenience Value

There are also reasons why some buyers in certain markets might pay more. One such reason is "convenience value"—the extra value that comes from a property in mint condition that in turn allows a buyer to move into a home one weekend and have a party the next.

In resort and second-home markets, like Lake Tahoe or Vail or the Hamptons of Long Island, properties sometimes trade with a substantial convenience value built in. This is due to the seasonal nature of the market. Someone buying a home in April does not want to wait six months for the keys to their house. They want to buy it, move in, and throw a party by the Fourth of July. In these markets, convenience value must be accommodated by adding an upward adjustment in core value calculations. Be aware that this is also a highly subjective adjustment and it, too, should always be stated in your assumptions and as a range.

Celebrity Value

Another reason why some buyers in some markets pay more is celebrity value. Usually this involves being able to say one owned "so and so's" house and enjoying the associated bragging rights that go along with it. While there is certainly a premium that will be paid, it is usually higher if the property is also in outstanding condition and well located and less if it is not so.

An Example of a Core Valuation Band

Let's synthesize all the above by imagining a property that is ten years old with 7,000 square feet on two acres of land, a swimming pool, a 500-foot driveway, and decent landscaping. I determine that a two-acre lot in the estate area is worth between $700,000 and $900,000, and that new luxury homes can be built for $250 to $350 per square foot. Pools run about $75,000 to $100,000 and the driveway runs about $70 to $90 per square foot ($35,000 to $45,000 for a 500-foot driveway).

Adding this up results in an initial core value as follows:

$700,000 to $900,000 for the lot +

$1,750,000 to $2,450,000 for the improvements +

$75,000 to $100,000 for the pool +

$35,000 to $45,000 for the driveway =

Reduce this value for the age of the improvements by, say, 25 percent for the ten years of age, or $447,500, to $612,500. For this property the core range of value is $2,112,500 to $2,882,500.

Invite the Seller to Participate

In the course of this exercise, invite the seller to participate with you by asking some questions, such as, *"What do you think the land is worth?" "How many square feet of improvements do you think you have here?" "What do you think it would cost today to rebuild the house?"*

(Her insurance agent should know the answer to the last question because the agent insures the house for replacement in the case of fire.)

This exercise should take only a few minutes. Remind your client that you are not looking for precision, but rather for a range. Explain that this is meant to replicate the kind of one-minute valuation that buyers and their agents will do in their head when viewing the property.

> Rarely will a buyer value a property at more than the replacement core value.

Finally, while you can suggest a discount for age, ask the client what discount she would apply if she were purchasing the home? In my example above of forty years, that works out to 2.5 percent per year. Over ten years it works out to 25 percent. The point here is that rarely will a buyer value a property at more than the replacement core value.

Doing this exercise with the client helps firmly ground her expectations. The client begins to see that price will not likely exceed replacement value. Why, after all, would anyone pay more for used goods? Your client also starts thinking the way many buyers and their agents think.

> When you are talking discount to core or 'book value,' you are talking the language of the luxury buyer. If you don't do these first two critical steps, you will never get a figure against which to apply a discount.

The resulting figure from these calculations is the estimated core value range. This is the step most agents never do. Usually agents go right to looking at past sales or looking at what's currently available, but there is a tremendous amount of value that you can usually ascertain by breaking down the components of the property and arriving at a "book" or core value. Most importantly, this core value is often a high figure that in turn can be discounted for our highly value-conscious buyers to represent the bargain they insist on always buying. And remember, when you are talking discount to core or "book value," you are talking the language of the luxury buyer. If you don't do these first two critical steps, you will never get a figure against which to apply a discount.

Step 3. Look to the Luxury Market for All Past Sales

Now you have an adjusted core value range. Next take that adjusted core value and compare it to other properties that have sold. Yes, I know I told you that there may not be much of a sold market. But here is what you can and should do: keep a list of every sale defined as luxury in your area (two to three times the average price). If I were to apply a multiple of, say, 2.5 to Greenwich that would be over $4.5M. In most of America it is over $1M. Whatever it is, keep the list and rank the sales by highest to lowest.

> Viewing a list of all past sales helps you and your client put value in perspective.

This instantly shows you (and your client) the whole market. Take your adjusted core value and insert it in these past sales to see how you fit in. Viewing that list helps you and your client put value into perspective. It provides no small comfort to your client that you know all the sales, so don't underestimate the importance of presenting this data to your client. It also allows you to ask such questions as, where might this property rank? Is it as good as the highest sale? If not, why not? How does it compare to the second highest sale? Keep moving down the list to see where this property fits in.

The list should include at least two years' worth of sales. If your area is in decline it should cover at least a year before the peak of the market, meaning the list could extend back five years or more.

How low a starting point to use will change with each market. You can certainly start out with properties that are less than two to three times the average price, but if the market is a highly liquid one, this may provide too much data. What is important is that it be accurate, and that it begin with the most expensive sale and work down from there.

While this sounds pretty simple, in reality it is not. While the list is relatively easy to put together in highly liquid markets like Beverly Hills, Palm Beach, Manhattan, and Greenwich, in other markets it can be very difficult to compose.

For instance, imagine pricing a horse farm with 420 acres in Virginia. It may be the only horse farm in the area for miles or there may be many but they are scattered all over the state. Your research may take you very far outside the specific town in which the property is located.

Or take the example of a ranch in Montana, Colorado, or Texas. These types of properties require a database and expertise far outside the local market. While that expertise is difficult to maintain, if you present to the seller all properties similar to theirs that have sold or are available in the multi-state region, the chances are good that you will get the listing. You have now provided them the focus and specialization they want in their agent and you are able to state the key words for getting a listing assignment: "I specialize in what you own."

Similarly, this kind of local and regional knowledge is valuable for waterfront properties. Knowing the price of waterfront footage in various markets allows you to value unique parcels. For instance, knowing the price per front foot of waterfront all around Cape Cod is an enormous advantage to a broker trying to secure a waterfront listing. Similarly, knowing the front foot rates for the intra-coastal waterways versus the ocean front rates in the Carolinas and in Florida, will distinguish you from 99% of all other agents in the market.

> The key words for getting a listing assignment: "I specialize in what you own."

Because markets are cyclical, you can often tell which phase the market is in by noting how much above or below the core value properties are trading. If several 7,000-square-foot home sales on two acres with a pool and decent landscaping have traded in a band between $3.5M to $4M and that is way above core value, you want to know that. It does not mean that you should decline the listing, but it simply indicates that properties are trading above their intrinsic, core, or book value at this phase in the cycle, often called the "overvaluation phase."

Step 4. What Else Is Available?

Fourth, look to see what else is currently available, i.e., the competition. Most agents are good at this. Pull all the data from the MLS or the database you keep and rank the offerings from highest asking price to lowest. This is the list you will provide the seller after your list of ranked past sales has been studied and fully absorbed. Ask about where the property might fall within these rankings and how it would compare to these offerings. After all, that is what the buyer will do.

Even for city properties where apartments are compared to others in the same building, consider how valuable it becomes to sellers and buying agents if you articulate how your city's asking prices (and your

> Begin with the most expensive sale and work down from there.

listing) also compare to London or Paris or Tokyo. Bringing this kind of perspective provides you a huge competitive edge. You then establish yourself as a local expert with a broader perspective.

Step 5. Look to Third Parties

There are several indicators of value from third parties that should be referenced during pricing. These are from entities that have also tried to determine the value of the property, such as the following:

Assessed Value This is what the local taxing authority thinks the property is worth for tax purposes. Since you need to know the taxes and therefore the assessed value, put this factor into the pricing mix.

Appraised Value Before going to the listing appointment, ask the seller if an appraisal has been done on the property. If not, it means that no one has enlightened the client to the property's value. If an appraisal exists, ask the seller to send over a copy before the meeting. If you get stiff objections to doing this, it may be a point worth discussing during the first meeting.

Do sellers of luxury property often have appraisals done? Yes and no. Often they are done for insurance purposes. After all, if the house burns down, the client needs to know the replacement value. Or she may have an appraisal done for the sake of a net worth statement.

If an appraisal has been done, it is important to obtain a copy. Regardless of how old it is, it will hold details relevant to assessing the property today. For example, just a description of the property will often reveal things you didn't know such as easements, rights of way, and deed restrictions.

Remember the title of this chapter is "No Fingers in the Air." You need to see if the appraiser did just that, i.e., stuck a finger in the air to arrive at value. If the appraisal is a good one, both you and your seller now know what every buyer will be seeing when they get the property appraised. If the appraisal is bad, its descriptions might still be useful to you. If the appraisal data is old but the methodology is accurate, adjust the numbers using recent appreciation rates in the area, or more recent sales. This, at a minimum, represents one less finger in the air and offers a better stab at the value of the property.

If there is no appraisal, ask the client if she intends to get one. It is possible she has never considered getting one. If she is open to having one done, it might be worth waiting to list the property until after its completion because one of the most fundamental questions, value through the eyes of an independent third party, awaits determination.

The Reasonable Businessperson Rule

Sometimes clients do not want to labor through a core value discussion, nor do they want to get an appraisal. Instead they may say, "I want this amount. Can you get it for me?"

Don't let this question stop you in your tracks. Do not say nothing or, worse, nod dutifully and then go back to your manager and say, "I just have to find that right buyer, that one in a million buyer." Most assuredly you will fail. Agents who do so mirror the folly of their sellers. Rather than being true advisers and knowledgeable market experts, which is what the seller hired them to be, they turn out to be only "yes" agents.

The reasonable businessperson rule helps you respond to such inquiries. It simply asks the question, "Will any reasonable businessperson pay what the seller expects?"

The proper response to the sellers is, "Mr. and Mrs. Seller, you didn't get to the point of owning such a fine property without being smart and sharp business people. You'll therefore understand when I tell you that the market is made up of sellers and buyers like yourselves. Buyers tend to be just as smart as sellers. They are cautious and value conscious."

> "Will any reasonable businessperson pay what the seller expects?"

Rich buyers hire advisers to make sure they don't make a mistake. Even if an impulse buyer were to fall in love with a property, he would go back to his lawyer, his accountant, his financial adviser, or trust officer and tell them what he has done. It is at this point that the voice of reason enters the picture. These advisers may now want to see the property. At a minimum they start asking key questions, beginning with a defense of value. They order an appraisal to be done on behalf of the buyer in order to establish what a reasonable person would pay. These people are all hired to protect the buyer from making a foolish decision like overpaying for a property. That is their job.

I can assure you that advisers will do this if for no other reason than to keep the funds that will be used to purchase this property from slipping out of their control (financial managers often get a 1 to 2 percent management fee). Releasing these funds may thus reduce their pay. They don't want to diminish their fees, so they will do whatever they can to prevent their client from overpaying.

Tell clients that they cannot avoid the reasonable businessperson rule. They will find this strategy used either on the buyers' side or from their advisers.

Ask clients to put themselves in the position of the buyer. Buyers want the very best value for their money. You have to present a defense of the value. Without it you may fail even to get them to see the property. An appraisal can provide the seller's defense in advance, but it can do so only if it is done by the seller.

Finally, if you find that the seller is still recalcitrant and will not accept the reasonable businessperson rule, then you have the buyer-agent issue.

Buyer-Agents

The real estate industry has changed dramatically over the past twenty years, from the use of sub-agency to the use of buyer agency in transactions. With buyer agency the agent for the buyer is looking out for and has a fiduciary responsibility to the buyer. With this dramatic change the lawyer, the counselor, the financial adviser, the trust officer, etc., have been institutionalized in the form of the buyer-agent whose primary fiduciary responsibility is to make sure that the buyer does not overpay for a property.

In fact, you need to inform your client that the buyer-agent is so concerned with preventing their client from making a foolish decision that he will do a comparative market analysis for the buyer prior to the purchase. The buyer-agent may also suggest that his client request an appraisal prior to purchase.

Buyer's Appraisal versus Seller's Appraisal

Whoever does the appraisal influences its result. When the sellers do the appraisal, they can create a valuation that is skewed to them rather than leaving the appraisal to the buyer's influence.

Remind the client that the buyer will want to add some leverage to the deal and take advantage of the deductibility of mortgage interest. If the buyer finances some part of the purchase, you are right back to getting an appraisal, only now it is for the bank or finance company.

Thus, reality bites the client three times: once by the CMA done by the buyer-agent, once by the appraisal the buyer-agent is sure to recommend, and a third time by the appraisal for the financial institution involved.

This means there is no escape from doing an appraisal. It is only a question of when it gets done and who influences it, the buyer or the seller.

On Bad Appraisals

What if the appraisal is based upon faulty reasoning, or worse, if it is done by someone hired by the seller to say what the seller wants? After all, there are appraisers who will say what the person who hires them wants said.

I think it is better to know this up front than to have the seller pull it out later in the negotiating process. Some agents shy away from this reality, spend a year on a listing, work themselves crazy determining the market value for the property, and then finally get an offer that is the best thing the seller will ever see. They present it, believing that finally they got the job done, only to be met by a rejection of the offer and no counter-offer because the seller pulls out an appraisal that says the property is worth a million more than the market.

That bad appraisal will not only kill the deal, but it will also do a disservice to your seller, who will likely lose the best shot at selling the property because they followed the appraisal's bad advice.

Step 6. Motivation as the Key to Successful Pricing

Understanding a seller's motivation is the sixth step in pricing and one of the keys to being successful in luxury real estate. The motivation of the seller is the single most important determinant of whether this seller will respond to the market you are creating. While there may be some valid reasons for dealing with unmotivated sellers (see why you might want to take an overpriced listing later in this chapter), do so knowing the risks in advance.

You have to qualify sellers for motivation just as you qualify buyers. You can have the best-priced property and create the most robust market with multiple bidders, but if the seller is not motivated, all is for naught. The opposite is also true. Even when dealing with a seriously overpriced property, If the seller is motivated, success is still possible.

In the luxury marketing business, an ideal listings mix is 80 percent of your sellers with acceptable motivation, and no more than 20 percent trophy properties or celebrity listings, which represent greater risk but provide your business a high profile cache.

When motivation is not clear, the question is whether the risk is worth the benefits of controlling those special properties. This 20 percent aside, the goal is to become an expert at recognizing seller motivation so that most of your time is spent marketing homes only for truly motivated sellers.

Each week, examine your portfolio of listed properties and assess client motivation to sell. If more than 20 percent of your listings have unclear motivations, stop. Get something sold or turn back the listing before you risk taking on another.

How to Determine Seller's Motivation

Because pricing is more difficult and less precise in luxury marketing, sellers almost always want to position themselves at the high end of the value range, which increases the risk to the marketing agent. If you are going to survive as a luxury real estate agent, you have to become very good at accurately guessing client motivation.

> You have to become very good at accurately guessing client motivation.

Agents ask me questions about determining seller motivation more often than any other. For this reason, I provide a list of motivations on my website just for agents.[17] Still, there is plenty to discuss here.

First, always take another agent to the listing presentation. This is because two agents can listen better than one. While one agent talks, the other can be more cognizant of body language changes or watch for other tip-offs by the seller. Even if the seller is a good friend and it seems somewhat awkward to have another person there, just introduce the second agent as part of the marketing team. The client should be happy that you cared enough to bring additional support.

Next, build a relationship with the sellers so they are comfortable enough to share. Here, too, having a second person helps tremendously. Two people provide a greater likelihood of striking up rapport.

The Four Personality Types

Ever since Hippocrates and the Roman physician Galen of Pergamun, humans have categorized people by personality types. The early twentieth century articulation of this came in 1909 from Rudolf Steiner, who divided people into the sanguine, melancholic, choleric, and phlegmatic. This categorization has been reincarnated for modern life into the Expressive, Analytical, Driver and Sociable personality types.[18]

These can provide clues on how to approach building a relationship with a client. If, for example, the agent is a Driver and the seller is a Sociable, there is little chance that the two can bond. But if a second agent goes on the listing who is a Sociable, there is a greater chance of rapport. Similarly, if the seller is an Analytical, bring along an associate who is an Analytical to cement the bond. Finding the bond that knits is the basis of trust, and trust will uncover motivation.

The Four Personality Types and their Compatibilities

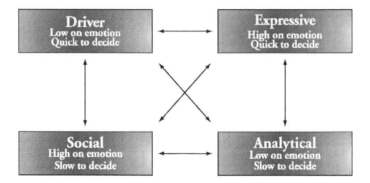

Ask Questions and Listen

Most agents have attended a listing pitch in which the seller just wants to talk about price. In these cases, it is usually fruitless to argue. Instead, let her demonstrate her knowledge about the market. This provides an excellent opportunity for you to listen and ask questions. Some sellers have followed the potential pricing for their property through local sales for years, knowing who bought what and when. Listen and benefit from their substantial time investment.

Ask for the Seller's Valuation

Such moments provide the chance to ask a bold question: "Would you price your home for me?"

In fact, before saying anything about value and pricing, ask the seller what they think the value of the property is. You can bet they have thought about it—a lot. Ask them, therefore, what they would price it at and why. Follow that up with what price they would pay if they were a buyer.

Asking these questions allows you to see how much they have thought about valuation and helps you understand their rationale. Remember, they know the property better than you ever will. When they provide a figure, encourage them to defend it by saying, "Pretend I am the buyer. Tell me how you arrived at that number." Don't be surprised if the seller has already drafted a good sales pitch.

After obtaining the sellers' opinion, work with them to compare their price to what buyers will be seeing in the market at that time. This is where

> If the seller is not motivated, all is for naught.

bringing out the spreadsheet with all available luxury properties ranked from most expensive to least is a great service. Ask the sellers to price their property and insert the price into the list. Where do they want to rank on a sheet of available properties?

Having allowed the seller both to educate you about their property and suggest a price, you have allowed them to be more open to taking your suggestions, rather than fighting them. Getting a seller to talk is an important way to learn about both the property and their motivations.

Help with Motivation from the Appraisal

Once you have an appraisal, sit down with the seller and review it. It is likely that he knows its contents inside and out. At a minimum, going over the appraisal represents an independent third party talking to the seller. In listening to the seller's reaction, you may better understand his motivation to sell. If the seller, for example, reacts negatively to a good appraisal, then you may be working with an unreasonable person who is just hoping you will find someone to make a foolish purchase. If so, pack up your things—this is not a seller you want to list.

Other Questions

Many good trainers in the marketplace today have lists of questions that help uncover motivation, including:

- "What is your reason for selling now?"
- "What is your timetable for sale?"
- "What if I brought you a full price offer in thirty days?"
- "Do you know where you will be moving to?"

One of my all time favorites is the Wide Open Question, the so-called Whooopen question: "In a perfect world, how would you like to see this whole process work?"

The key motivators are several:

- Death, disease, divorce, disability, and desire.
- Relocation to a new job.
- Promotion or a big new job. (Here sellers need a new house to meet their new standing in the community, at work, or in the social hierarchy of the rich. This is a strong motivator.)
- Life/family issues such as starting a family, having more children, or parents moving in.

There are other questions to ask and motivations to watch out for. See my book *Winning Listing Presentations,* the bulk of which is made up of the questions you need to ask to win a listing. In that book I argue that this list of questions serves as the core of your listing presentation because no one cares how much you know until they know how much you care. Asking questions shows that you care and helps you to build rapport with your seller. In addition, by listening to answers you can better discern their motivation. An arsenal of questions allows you to have a vibrant and productive conversation with your client and that conversation is the best listing presentation.

Does Super-Motivated Mean Lower Price?

With a highly motivated seller, it is common to price a property low to get it sold quickly.

In estate sales where cash must be raised quickly to pay estate taxes, this may well be the right strategy. In these cases, low pricing should bring multiple bidders and a quick sale—if that is what the seller wants. But don't deceive yourself into believing you got the highest price; it is low pricing that got the buyers into the game, not competitive *power marketing* expertise.

But in some circumstances, super motivation allows the opposite. For some super-motivated sellers, you can price properties more aggressively because you know they are going to sell. Whenever the seller will take the best offer that your *power marketing* produces, you can engage in riskier pricing because other risks have been lowered due to strong seller motivation. By doing this, you may not only get more for the seller, but you may also acquire a client or referral source for life.

Step 7. Setting the Asking Price

Now that you've determined core value, adjusted it for all the variables, correlated it to past sales to see if properties are selling above or below it, compared it to currently available properties in the market, told the seller the high and low range of likely valuation, articulated a credible, defensible value, and determined motivation, it's time to settle on the asking price.

> The prior discussion of motivation bears directly on setting the asking price; if you have a highly motivated seller, price at the upper end of the valuation range. If you have a seller whose motivation is less than stellar, price at the lower end of the range. Similarly, if you are in an up market with prices rising steadily, price at the higher end of the band. If you are in a down market, focus more on the core value versus past sales, and make sure you have a defensible value for the market and its buyers.

Steps 1 to 6 of this process should now make Step 7 easy. The proper asking price should come into view as you move through the process. In the end, pricing must be high enough that sellers do not feel they are leaving money on the table, but it must be credible and defensible enough to attract agents and buyers.

Finally, the asking price of a property is like a lure on a fishing line: if it doesn't attract any fish, change the lure. The asking price is only as good as the buyers it attracts.

7 Steps in Pricing Luxury Homes

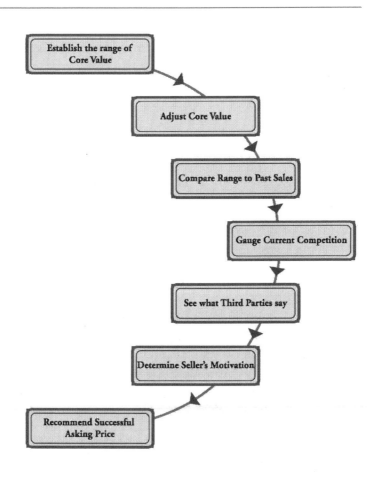

The Whole Process in One Story (and then Some)

When I was manager of a Greenwich real estate office, one of my agents came with a property he wanted to list for $6.95M. Because the agent did not have much experience in this price range, I asked for some history. He told me it had been listed with a national competitor for a year —without any offers.

The agent sensed my hesitation and grew a little tense. I knew he wanted to demonstrate his ability to list a property in this price range. But it was also office policy to front all the risk of taking such a listing. I knew that as long as the agent did not have to risk any money marketing the property, he would be happy to take it for the prestige of the listing and let me worry about the cost.

The agent asked me for a marketing plan to see what we would be prepared to spend. I demurred and said it should await a meeting with the seller and a determination of price.

"What about price?" I asked. He provided a disheartening and weak rationale.

"Look, on properties like this there is no defense of value. Either someone falls in love with it or not. That is it."

The hairs on the back of my neck started to stand tall. He had said the worst that could be said to any manager. His was the roulette argument, that listing real estate is just a big gamble and if someone hits the number, it sells. Needless to say, this did not have any traction with me.

"So tell me, what is there to fall in love with here?"

He proceeded to give an uninspiring portrait of the property.

The main house had been a barn within which the current owners had created a non-traditional floor plan. Several agents who had seen it thought it was an "upside-down house" because the kitchen and dining room were in the basement, but at least the basement was a walk out that overlooked the pool (currently under reconstruction, it looked a mess, but assuredly it would be all back together soon). There were twenty acres of lovely property, but the owner raised bees as a hobby so buyers were reluctant to walk around for fear of getting stung. Near the children's play area, the owners kept a family of ducks, a goat, some sheep, and Henrietta, the pet pig, who on two occasions oinked loudly during showings and once got out of her pen.

I said nothing, but suggested that this required not only a meeting with the owner but also an in-depth tour of the property with them. From my point of view we had to start at the beginning.

The agent left with no doubt that I would nix his chance to list a major property and break into the big leagues. My work was cut out for me.

It was compounded by another agent in the office who alerted me that the listing had been turned down by my predecessor manager as an overpriced waste of time. She added that people in the office were pleased that our competitors had gotten it. They expected it would fail to sell and were vindicated by the fact that it had languished for a year on the market.

The agent—it seemed—was working on a different agenda: increasing his status in the community by having his name attached to a $6M listing. While there is value in having and controlling prestigious listings, listing overpriced properties is the easiest game in town and the quickest way to go broke.

My goal for the office was to sell 90 percent of the properties we listed by listing fewer, but more saleable properties—leaving the listing game to other offices.

The Consequences of Not Having Defensible Value

I imagined how this would all play out. At showings the young agent would grope for an adequate defense of value (as he had done in my office). As he was beaten down by the market and other agents, his enthusiasm for the listing would wane. He would demand more and more advertising to cover his mistake and blame his company for not supporting him. He would keep saying to himself, his client, and his manager that we "just have to find the right buyer."

As his manager, I would also lose by signaling to others in the office that I was willing to spend time and money on overpriced listings. Other agents who had well-priced listings would get discouraged by my wasting money on this kind of property. And ultimately, the agent would fail his seller because he could not defend value. His status would decline, not increase.

Fortunately, this story had a happy outcome. My questioning of the agent led him to come back into my office and show me a plot plan of the property. He indicated that during the first offering the property had been presented on twenty acres. This time around, the seller was offering thirty acres; in this market, picking up ten acres was gold.

When I asked him about the subdivision potential, I learned that the best local engineering firm had come up with a subdivision plan carving out six two-plus-acre lots, each worth about $700,000, and one 5.75-acre lot with the main house and outbuildings on it that was worth about $1 million. In addition, the engineering firm had a plan to put twelve acres into permanent conservation, which added more value to the main house and several of the two-acre lots.

This meant that there was now $5.2M in core land value before factoring in the improvements. I asked how big the house was and he said about 8,000 square feet. At that time a replacement value of $150 a foot was generous, but not out of line. Adding that amount yielded another $1.2M of improvement value, which brought the valuation to $6.4M or within 10 percent of the $6.95M proposed asking price.

We had cleared the first hurdle: creating a thirty-second defensible articulation of value

Adding in the pool, guest and pool houses, garages, and driveway, might easily add another $200,000 of value, which brought the total to $6.6M. This dramatically improved my comfort level.

Suddenly, a failed listing looked a lot more interesting and I was eager to get involved. There were still many other steps, but we had cleared the first hurdle: creating a thirty-second defensible articulation of value. We arranged to meet the owner and see the house.

The house was interesting from the outside and had many of the elements needed to get a high price. No one could tell that it had once been a barn. Instead, the owner had installed a Mt. Vernon-style pillared front and proper entry gates done with stone supports.

But inside, the house was disappointing. It was indeed an upside-down house, designed and decorated for the current family's use. It had all the charm—including the wear and tear—of a family home. It lacked that decorator-type retail magic that often lures buyers to buy. To the owner's credit, it was clear that this was a well-loved house, not meant to be a museum.

However, once on the market, it would be compared to the glitz of the competition and that meant that buyers and their agents' eyes would wander. Also, my initial valuation of $150 per square foot was not, in short, a reasonable defense of value, since for that figure, one could build a fine new home. Thus, despite my initial favorable defense of value, we had to adjust the $150 per square foot figure to just $100. This reduced the valuation by $350,000. Now we were at $6.25M on a 6.95M ask.

Here is where meeting an owner and assessing motivation is so critical. First, the seller owned four companies and had an acute sense of value. He had thought through the sale of this important asset very clearly. He personally worked on the subdivision plan, got it approved through the town's planning department, and was able to articulate the resulting value.

As it turns out, it was a good plan, full of flexibility for him as an owner and for us as his marketers. The owner knew every inch of his property and insisted we check out the guts of the house and property, something of which he was very proud. Touring the property, we noticed the tremendous—and readily apparent—infrastructure costs that he had absorbed.

He had, for instance, installed extensive outdoor drains that would cost $100,000 to install today. There was a $70,000 septic system, a mile of roads that would cost $40,000; an internal hot water system worth $20,000; an emergency generator for the entire property for $100,000; an air-conditioning system priced at $40,000; landscaping worth $180,000; a greenhouse, guest houses, pool house, all easily adding another $250,000.

Suddenly, value was everywhere. It just was not obvious and needed to be highlighted and marketed—something that had not been done by the first listing broker.

I grew excited about the listing and about working with such a thoughtful and meticulous owner. At the end of our tour, we came up with $5.2M for the land, $800,000 for the house, and $780,000 of infrastructure, totaling $6.78 million of value.

But in our market there was an additional premium we had not included: the rarity value of the property, which consisted of the ability to buy such a large piece of land already subdivided. Where sub divisible land was hard to come by, a property like this could be counted as part of one's financial portfolio. It was likely to go up in value far more than either inflation or the stock market. The subdivided lots were truly an investment for any buyer, who could retain the main house as a luxury home.

> You can be the most aggressive in pricing with super-motivated sellers (if they wish) because they will either take a lower price if necessary or quickly adjust their asking price.

I believed the rarity value was high enough to command a 15 percent premium to core value. The high rarity premium provided cover for a situation in which the buyer wanted to tear down the house. For this reason, we took out the house altogether.

By taking out any value for the house, we destroyed the objection that someone might have to tear it down. Even doing this we could defend value because of the 15 percent rarity premium. Our core value was $5.2 million for the land, $780,000 of amenities and 15 percent premium for investment rarity value, which gave us a core valuation of almost $6.9M without anything ascribed to the house. In effect, we were throwing the impressive main house in for free.

Now we had an immensely saleable property, owned by a reasonable, rational owner, with clear, credible, and defensible value. Agents and buyers would be instantly more comfortable—as was I in my role as manager.

We left the property going over the intrinsic value, excited about our seller, delighted at the listing and the chance to do what our competition had not done.

Not only did we now have a listing worthy of our time and money, but I had an agent who had learned a valuable lesson that could be applied to other properties. He now understood defensible value. His productivity would now increase. I was also excited because I sensed a $6M + sale.

▲ ▲ ▲

Having now completed the seven steps to pricing luxury properties, I can't leave this chapter without two final discussions: aggressively priced listings and a reminder of how you can provide additional value to get record prices.

When to Take an Aggressively Priced Listing

Some very good agents in luxury marketing will blame me for teaching you to overprice listings, which can really screw up the market. While I realize this risk, the simple fact is that the luxury end of the market is full of "overpriced" listings—it always has been and always will be.

This section grew out of a bad day I had at my firm. My partner and our director of career development, had invited me to one of our training classes in which the new agents walked through their listing presentations. We sat in a simulated living room as agents rang a pretend doorbell and walked in to pitch us on listing a $2.4M apartment. They were to demonstrate that they knew their scripts and could deliver them with the proper enthusiasm and conviction.

I sat for presentation after presentation. I liked their professionalism, their handshakes, and energy. I thought their CMAs were relatively good and were backed by solid market research. However, I walked away from that class believing that I would not list my property with any of them. Worse, I felt the same way about the last class, in which the agents had done stellar presentations but in only one case would I have considered listing my property.

Why? Because none of them demonstrated to me the willingness to take some risks to get an aggressive price; instead, they did a good job of telling me what had sold in the area and then, based upon those sales, explaining what the apartment was worth. They didn't show any confidence in their ability to get me the highest price.

While my team was noticeably disturbed by my reaction, I got everyone even more nervous when I

> While there is value in having and controlling prestigious listings, listing overpriced properties is the easiest game in town and the quickest way to go broke.

argued that there was a time and a place to be more aggressive with pricing. Because it is such a sensitive topic, it became clear that I had to write this section and try to offer some guidance on why and when to take aggressively priced listings. So here goes.

Some of the reasons to take an aggressively priced luxury listing include:

- *Rising prices* Prices are rising in the market, and you have to anticipate what things will sell for, not what they sold for in the past.

- *Little competition* There is little competition for this particular property and not likely to be much in the future.

- *Strong motivation* The sellers are very motivated, and although they want a high asking price, they will take a more reasonable one.

- *Unique* You have no idea how much the property is worth, and the only way to find out is to determine core value, create a valuation range, gauge motivation, then utilize the kind of *power marketing* described here.

- *Defensible value* You are able to articulate a credible, defensible reason for a buyer to pay the high price.

- *Pricing leader* You want to be a pricing trendsetter, always pushing the envelope on pricing.

- *Set new benchmarks* There is no finer credential than a record sale; when there is a possibility for one, you should grab it.

- *No comparables* There is nothing else like it on the market. Maybe it is the last piece of waterfront in this town. Or maybe it is a large chunk of land that has rarity value as I described above.

- *Good listing terms* You can get the property on listing terms that will reduce your risk, like a long listing period with compensation for marketing costs.

- *Automatic price adjustments* You can list the property at X price but you have a price reduction written right into the listing agreement that kicks in every thirty days. So armed, you can then "test" the market, but you also are sending a positive message every thirty days by reducing the price automatically.

- *Gain market presence* You are establishing market share or market presence and you need a listing to do it. This reason is the most dangerous because it can be used to rationalize taking anything and at prices that do your reputation more harm than good. So be careful.

- *Celebrity sale* It has celebrity value, historical value, or notoriety value that is hard to quantify but adds to its allure and market value.

White House Orders

My former colleague at LandVest, Jim Retz, had the distinction while working at Previews in California to list the Pacific Palisades home of President and Mrs. Ronald Reagan. At the time this was surely the most exciting celebrity property in the country, as the Reagan's had already moved into the White House. In his enthusiasm to work with the First Family, Jim agreed upon a price from a presidential adviser that, as Jim says, "was considerably higher than we felt it was worth." A year later Jim sold the property "for considerably less than our original price." Nonetheless, Jim got the listing, the sale, and most importantly the bragging rights for a lifetime.

> Jim got the listing, the sale, and most importantly the bragging rights for a lifetime.

While your reputation needs to be grounded in selling luxury real estate and not taking overpriced listings, to engage in luxury marketing you have to set an image of pricing leadership. You should always want to have the most expensive listings in your market. If you do not set aggressive prices, you will never control the inventory nor get the well-priced listings.

About Letting It Pass

Sometimes it is better to let another agent take an overpriced listing. Tell the owner that you cannot justify the pricing the seller wants (something better done in person) and stress how important it is for the seller to be with someone who can be enthusiastic about the sale.

There is a saying that it is better to be someone's first love, second wife, and third real estate agent. Sometimes it is best to wait for the listing to come back to you.

Bringing the One Buyer (and the Accompanying Danger of Doing So)

Sometimes sellers ask that you bring buyers with whom you're currently working to their property. If you work only with sellers, just say that you specialize in working with sellers and marketing listings and, therefore, do not have any buyers. But if, like most agents, you work with both sellers and buyers, it is possible that you know a perfect buyer for this house.

One way to handle this is let your buyer agent (if you have one) take the buyer in. Alternatively, the buyer can be given to another trusted agent in the office, and then you take a referral fee (possibly as high as half the selling commission).

To do anything else is perilous for a listing broker. One of the most powerful things you can say to sellers is that you specialize in selling what they own. Trying to be a luxury listing agent and a selling agent in the same market violates this fundamental principle.

One Buyer Is Not in the Client's Interest

However, as discussed at the opening of Chapter 4, it simply is not in the client's interest to have one buyer. While not bringing the buyer to the property means you risk missing a sale, in reality the buyer (as the only buyer for that a property) will bid low, and there probably will be no sale anyway.

What is more certain is that there will be huge disappointment on the part of the seller that the buyer did not buy. The seller will remember you for the low-ball offer you produced rather than associating you with getting the highest price. The seller will recall that you compromised everything you said in the living room about multiple buyers bidding simultaneously to bend to the desire to show "just this one buyer." Worse, the seller will not come back to list the property with you. By succumbing to the seller's initial request, you lose credibility and do no real service for the seller.

Do not try to burn the candle at both ends. Be what you are, a marketer and a listing broker—not a buying broker. If you must refer them to another competent buyer's broker, take a hefty referral fee, and let them deal with the seller. You will get something for the effort while keeping your integrity and reputation intact for future listings and sales.

Getting Record Prices

Getting record prices is the icing on the real estate cake for *power marketers*. Big sales and high prices are part of the ethos of the luxury real estate world. Holding a record for the highest price is the golden stamp of approval—and the best reason for a seller to hire you.

Down Market Blues

Getting a record price in a down market is very difficult, if not impossible. I once tried to do this in October 1987, by bringing to market one of the most expensive properties in the United States, "Harbour Point" on Center Island in Oyster Bay, New York.

Priced at $26M, the property consisted of a main house plus eight other buildings on a twenty-five-acre waterfront peninsula, within a gated community, abutting nearly thirty acres of conservation land. It had all the makings of a record sale.

The day before my Tuesday open house the stock market crashed, falling 22 percent in a single day. On that grim Tuesday morning, I welcomed brokers to Harbour Point feeling rather ill. All I could do was pretend that the world had not changed the day before. But it had. I was now trying to market something for which the possibility of success was slim to none. Even worse, my sellers were extremely upbeat and confident in my ability to market their property.

In the end, I did produce an $18M cash offer for the property, which my sellers did not accept, as their expectations had been too high. The market did not fully recover for six years, during which time the listing expired, and they chose not to re-list the property. The property is said to have transferred for below our original listing price. So much for my valiant effort to score a record sale during a down market.

While there are occasions in down markets when getting a record sale is possible, this usually involves properties with huge celebrity or rarity value. Even then, down markets create an atmosphere of bargain hunting. Record-seeking in a discount environment is simply not worth your time.

Ingredients for Setting a Record Price

Property Amenities

+

Highly Motivated Seller

+

Right Market

+

Good Luck

+

Multiple Buyers

= Record Price

The Pleasures of Up Markets

During up markets, you should always be focused on getting record prices. In 1993 Robert Wilder and Bill Andruss of the Coldwell Banker office in Greenwich listed and sold the highest sale in Greenwich history, a twelve-acre waterfront estate that once belonged to Boss Tweed of Tammany Hall fame, and was subsequently owned by the Benedict family (whose cook happened to invent Eggs Benedict at the estate).

> Holding a record for the highest price paid in the market is the golden stamp of approval—and the best reason for a seller to hire you.

That sale propelled Bill to become one of the preeminent luxury brokers in Greenwich. While he had been a successful agent before that sale, thereafter he exclusively focused on the prime estate market in Greenwich. He still holds a position as one of the top luxury agents in the country.

What You Need to Set Records

Getting record prices requires several preconditions. Both Harbour Point and the Benedict estate had the right mix of qualities, including waterfront, a large land parcel, abutting conservation land, a pedigree or history, views, and location in a premier luxury community. They also had celebrity value or rarity value. But one became unsalable because we were entering a recession, and the other sold because we were coming out of one.

Second, the property requires a highly motivated seller who is willing to engage with you in getting that price.

> One became unsaleable because we were entering a recession, and the other sold because we were coming out of one.

I cannot overemphasize the need for a cooperative and solid working relationship between seller and broker.

Third, the timing must be right, preferably an up market with solid liquidity. With all these conditions in place for a record sale, you still need one more: you must use *power marketing* to create a situation in which multiple buyers bid simultaneously on the property.

How to Add Value for the Client

I will end this pricing chapter with several important actions that allow you to get high prices, record prices, or even just get a property sold in a bad market.

No discussion of pricing is complete for *power marketers* without understanding how to create value by spurring competition. In this world, the price your clients receive is determined by the quality of the marketing you provide.

Create urgency to act with these advance actions

You now know where we are trying to get our clients: that moment in time when we have multiple buyers bidding simultaneously or the threat thereof. To get there we have to create an urgency to act. There is no better way to create urgency to act than by creating the groundwork on which competition can sprout. So the first thing we want to do is have our seller take three specific actions that will set them on the road to success. These actions are designed directly to eliminate any buyer stall; to eliminate anything that will prevent bidding.

1. *Appraisal:* The buyer or the buyer agent will get an appraisal and use it against you, so your client needs to get one and have it ready to provide buyers. It is critical that your client knows in advance what the appraiser will say.

2. *Home inspection*: By having it done in advance, no buyer can feign delay awaiting one. It can be handed them and eliminate any stall. If they want their own, fine, but don't let that be a condition of sale. Remember we want to create urgency to act.

3. *Title Search:* Eliminate any issue with title by having your client's attorney have it all ready.

By eliminating these roadblocks, we have eliminated three reasons to wait and greatly enhanced the chances of having competitive bids. All the bidders have been put on the same playing field with the same information so that everyone can bid together and focus on the price they are going to pay, not whether it will appraise out or whether the roof leaks or whether there are any title issues.

When we get our seller to do these things in advance, we position them for getting the highest price.

Who Might Bid the Highest: The Case of Abutters

In my experience, sometimes the highest bidder for a property is literally right next door. Abutters are a classic case of generating a high price based upon excellent value. Here is how.

I always ask sellers if I can contact their neighbors to introduce myself and let them know what is going on with the property—even if the sellers have already done so. Abutters—like most neighbors—always want to know what is going on. Since the sale can affect their value, they also have an interest in seeing the property sell for a good price, and sometimes they are the buyer who can best afford to pay it.

The reason abutters often have the willingness to pay the most is that their property, when combined with your listing, provides greater value than each property valued separately. For instance, when someone has three-quarters of an acre of land in a half-acre zone and can buy the property next door, which also has three-quarters of an acre, they can get three half-acre lots out of the two parcels and thereby create extra land value. That means a listing may be worth more to the abutter because he or she has something that increases the value of the property to them.

The same is true with vertical living in condo towers, as in Manhattan or Miami Beach. If an adjacent apartment (above or below) comes to market, the value to neighbors in owning additional bedrooms or space is greater than to the outside world. Abutters are often the most emotional and impulsive of buyers, having the most to gain and to lose.

First Offers Can Be Record Offers

The second group of buyers that can help you to get record prices are first offerers. Every real estate agent knows that a buyer's first offer is often his best. First offers often come from buyers who have been on the market for awhile and already know that nothing else fits their desires.

They are prepared to act more quickly because they are afraid of losing, which drives them to bid aggressively, too.

With both abutters and first offerers, the threat of other buyers creates their urgency to act. Because of this they offer an outstanding opportunitty for securing a high price and need to be coddled and encouraged as much as possible.

How to Create Competition

Create a defensible, credible value
↓
Call abutters
↓
Expose property to all agents
↓
Use media: Internet, direct mail, social media, etc.
↓
Have synchronized showings
↓
Make everyone aware of offers
↓
Use print ads to catalyze interests
↓
Make the 'last call' to all agents
↓
Orchestrate multiple bidders, simultaneously

Making the Last Call

Making the last call is the tried and true means of getting the highest price in any market at any time and in any price range. In luxury marketing, it is the one essential *power marketing* action step above all others that will achieve the highest price the market will bear. Let's review what the last call is all about.

When you have offers on a property and feel a deal may be near, make the last call; you (as the listing agent) should call all the agents who have expressed interest in the property and inform them that now there is "serious buyer interest." You ask them if their buyers are still interested. If so, inform them that they need to come forward now or lose the property. You are being the auctioneer here, giving everyone fair warning that in your opinion something is about to happen. You are respecting the buyers' desire to have a last shot and you are virtually guaranteeing that as you come to the finale of the sale, it will be completed through a competitive process. If there is no further interest, you will have at least exhausted all the possibilities, and your seller can rest comfortably knowing that you have pushed the market to its limit. Only now, after having made the last call, will you get your client to that goal of multiple buyers bidding simultaneously or the threat thereof. Only now have you completed your marketing and fiduciary responsibilities.

Making the last call almost always results in second or third showings to buyers who saw it once. If nothing else, they come back "just to make sure the property is not for us."

Most buyer agents appreciate this call because they know that buyers often wait to act until someone else is interested. They appreciate having a reason to call their buyers and alert them that a property in which they expressed interest may no longer be available. It further helps buyer agents convey to their clients that markets are moving. They appreciate your providing them this courtesy call. As mentioned before, it is buyers not receiving this call that infuriates them enough to complain to the manager's office.

> Making the last call results in activity or a buzz around a property.

I am not advocating shopping anyone's offer. That would be breaching confidential information and it would only anger both the agent and their buyer. It goes without saying that, as a credible and honorable agent, you should never make this call without really having "serious interest."

Making the last call not only results in activity or a buzz around a property, if I had my druthers, instituting the last call should be a new article of the Code of Ethics for the National Association of Realtors and be required of every sale before a final offer is accepted. Very little generates more value for a seller than making the last call and nothing confirms for all parties the fairness of the process where everyone has had a chance to bid, just like in the auction.

I vividly recall a situation in which a Greenwich agent, my wife Linda, had a $1.27M listing on which she had little to no activity. The sellers were not only close friends, but had already moved to California for a job transfer. They were sitting with a vacant house, desperate to sell.

After months of showings but no offers, Linda finally got a $975,000 offer on the property. She called the sellers, who were so eager to sell they were prepared to take the offer. But she told them to wait while she called all eighteen agents who had shown the property and told them that there was now serious interest. Within two days there were five additional showings, three buyers who had seen it before, and two new buyers generated by the buzz of activity. The result was a new bid for $1.025M. She then received a succession of bids, which after several weeks of negotiations, resulted in the seller getting $1.21M for the property. The last call resulted in her client receiving more than $200,000 above the first bid for the property (almost 25 percent more than the first offer).

This is the value added by *power marketing*. This is how price is a function of marketing. This is how we get the highest price and, sometimes, record prices. This is also how we maintain the highest ethic in our business and fulfill our fiduciary responsibilities. Finally, this is how we present the competition to buyers, liberate them from fear of bidding, unleash the desire to win, and, because of the transparency and inherent fairness of the process, also keep them happy.

The Takeaway _____

Luxury pricing is highly elastic, difficult to assess, and never fixed. The Seven Step process to arrive at an asking price is:

1   **Establish a range of core (book) value** for the property based upon the formula:

    Land + Replacement Cost Reduced by Obsolescence and Age + Amenities = Range of Core (Book) Value

2   **Adjust the core value range** for factors that add value and others that limit value. Add any "convenience value" or "celebrity value."

3   **Compare this range to past sales** to see where it places the property and make any additional adjustments based upon those sales.

4   **Compare the range to** other properties currently on the market to determine where your pricing should be positioned *vis* a vis those other possible purchases.

5   **See what third parties say about value**, such as the assessors and appraisers. Remind your clients that buyers are just as smart as sellers and tend to follow a reasonable businessperson rule. Recommend the seller get an appraisal before the buyer does.

6   **Assess your seller's motivation** to determine an asking price within the core value range. Always ask questions and bring a second person to your listing appointment to help you to determine motivation.

7   **Set the asking price with the seller**, informing her of the risk and rewards of the high and low range of core value. The asking price is only as good as the buyers it attracts.

While tradition forces you to have asking prices, your goal should be the creation of a market that can deliver the highest price, whether that is above or below the asking price.

Overpriced listings abound in luxury markets and carry risks, but are sometimes acceptable and even necessary. To be a luxury player one has to become adept at knowing when to take one and when to pass.

- Avoid the trap of a seller asking you to bring just one buyer. The buyer will not likely pay up because he will not have the necessary competition. As a result, you will likely lose the seller as a client.

- Getting record prices is most likely in an up market, but in any market you can garner value-added dollars for your clients by orchestrating first offerers, abutters, and most importantly, by making the last call.

- The price the seller gets is a function of the marketing (and marketer) chosen.

6

Finding Buyers and Qualifying Them

There are essential activities all luxury agents need to perform to get buyers. This chapter will explore the tools at your disposal to find them. Because much in this chapter will be familiar, I will focus primarily on what is not so apparent, the "Why?" behind using these tools and different ways in which you can and should use the same actions. I will end with how to qualify buyers.

What tools should you use? The best answer is as many as possible. Which are appropriate for the luxury market? Many can't be pinned down without dating this book because in reality they are always changing and often vary with local markets. But here is one that is not likely to change.

The All-Important, Vital, Powerful, Indispensable Other Agents

Occasionally, listing agents have been known to exclude other brokers and agents from selling a listing. This is the biggest mistake you as a *power marketer* can make. Because of the small size of the luxury market, you need all the help and exposure you can get from the brokerage community. There is a 90-95 percent chance the buyer will come through another agent. You never know from where (or which agent). Your most important marketing action is to include all agents and encourage their participation. Never exclude anyone.

Some luxury agents may include everyone reluctantly only because MLS rules require it. Others view the agents attending their MLS open houses as curiosity seekers who will never have a serious buyer.

You must never deviate from exposing a property to as many agents as possible. This means not just utilizing your local MLS or regional MLS; it means going out to national websites and actively noting who the luxury agents are and creating your own database of their emails. You should constantly be adding to this database and emailing your listings to these agents. If nothing else, doing so will keep your name front and center for referral business. But because of the interconnectedness of the rich, it is likely that a buyer for your property is sitting in the hands of an agent who is very far away from your market.

The point is that whether the buyer is far away or near, everyone should always be included.

case study ▼▼▼

Of Shabby Chic Real Estate Agents

The story of Sunninghill Farm in Brookville, New York should settle any issue about marketing a listing to everyone. This estate was the home of the co-owners of Seattle Slew, the famous Triple Crown racehorse who sired Slew of Gold and numerous other champion racehorses. The estate sat on twenty-eight gorgeous acres in a two-acre zone with easy access to expressways to New York City. I listed the property for $6.5M when I was still a rookie luxury agent honing my luxury marketing skills.

One Sunday afternoon I received a call from an agent on the North Shore of Long Island whose name I did not recognize. She told me that there was a man in a long stretch limousine outside her office who had seen our brochure for the property and wanted a showing that afternoon.

I asked her if she had pre-qualified him and she said that she had never met him before. I told her that I was sorry but all customers had to be pre-qualified and my sellers needed advance warning of a showing.

She asked me to hold the line. She went to the back of her office and whispered into the phone receiver that she really didn't know how to pre-qualify someone like this. But, she persisted, if the man wants to see a property, why couldn't he? She added that he was there right now and the property was just a mile down the road.

I told her that if she would allow me talk to him, I would attempt to begin the pre-qualification. She agreed.

I learned that he was a Wall Street investment manager. I told him that I hoped he understood that we could not arrange a showing without a banking reference and at least two other references.

He, in turn, said that he understood and it was no problem.

He gave me his banker's number and that of his lawyer and indicated that if I called his firm, there would be someone there today to verify who he was.

"But this is a Sunday," I said. "How can I call your banker today?"

He then indicated that the number he provided me was his banker's home number. In addition, he offered to call his banker to alert him to expect my call.

The banker was the president of the bank. He asked me how much the property was listed for, after which he confirmed that this gentlemen could well afford this property. I also called the buyer's attorney, and he confirmed the buyer was who he had said he was. He also said it would be no problem for this buyer to buy this property and pay all cash. Similarly, I called his office to confirm his employment.

He was the CEO.

Within a half hour I called him back and confirmed that everything checked out, and while it still might not be possible to arrange a last-minute showing, I would, nonetheless, try.

Fortunately, the owners were away and the caretaker said the house was in its usual immaculate condition, and there would be no problem showing it on such short notice. Next I called our showing agent, who lived locally, to see if she could be there. She could.

We showed it, and after several weeks of negotiations involving several other buyers, this gentleman ended up being the winning bidder.

A little while later I called the selling agent to congratulate her on producing the buyer. I asked if I could stop by her office and thank her in person. She agreed to meet at the same office where the buyer had come that fateful Sunday.

What I found was a large vacant lot overgrown with weeds on a corner of a state highway just off Interstate 495. Obviously the buyer had turned off the Interstate and headed to the estate district, stopping in at the first real estate office he saw. But this "office" looked like a small shack. It was no larger than the size of a backyard tool shed. In it was one desk with two chairs in front. That was it, except for one thing that caught my eye.

In the window was the color brochure of Sunninghill Farm we had sent all the agents. The broker/owner/sole agent had put the brochure in the window both to attract attention and possibly to suggest that it was her listing. At a minimum she wanted her firm to be associated with listings of this caliber.

It did not matter to us. We were always delighted for anyone to use our brochures for window dressing. All we cared about was finding as many buyers as possible.

That office remains in my memory to this day because it exemplifies how we never know from where a buyer will come. It was a one-woman show. Here was an office through which no one would ever have thought a $6M-plus buyer would have found his dream home, but he did.

Marketing Asset: How Other Agents View You

One of your most important tools for finding buyers is your good relations with other agents. A good relationship with other agents is a prerequisite for finding the buyers who work with those other agents. Don't believe me?

How many sales have been lost because someone didn't trust or want to work with the listing agent? Answer: more than the real estate profession is willing to admit. If you're in the industry, chances are you know an agent from hell with whom you cringe at the thought of working, who doesn't return phone calls, makes showings difficult, tries to end run you to your buyer, isn't straightforward with facts, and simply tries to keep other agents out of the deal. Such an agent hurts their seller by making it difficult for other agents. Your good standing and respect among agent peers is a vital asset that you bring to marketing a seller's property and attracting buyers to it. Preserve and protect that standing at all times. There is no commission worth your integrity.

To demonstrate your value to your clients, get testimonials from other agents in the business and include these on your personal marketing brochures and your website. Yes, testimonials from former clients are important, but think of how powerful testimonials from your peers can be.

> There is no commission worth your integrity.

You also must resolve the fear that you may not have the ultimate buyer for a listing sitting in your contact management system. Get over thinking that sellers choose you based on whether they believe you have the buyer. True, some do choose an agent this way, but only when they believe that the agent has nothing to offer other than a buyer in their back pocket.

You now have much more to offer. You are a *power marketer* who understands the vital orchestration role you play. Your job is not to have *one buyer*, but to bring in *all the buyers* in the marketplace through the solid relationships you enjoy in the brokerage community. The primary reason to hire you is to find all buyers, get them 'in the room' at the same time, raise their comfort level to bid, and then control the psychology of the sale to effectuate the highest price by getting two or more to bid simultaneously. That is what your seller needs and what you can offer. Once you have confidence in this *power marketing* skill, you will welcome agents (and their buyers) all into the room. The more bidders the better.

> Your job is not to have the buyer, but to find ALL the buyers.

The Many Reasons for Never Taking a "Quiet" Listing

Almost every real estate agent has faced sellers who say they do not really want to be on the market and instead just want a "quiet" listing without much hoopla. That means they don't really want the other agents in town to know they are thinking of selling. They just want you to bring them a buyer and they will make a deal. Welcome to the world of sellers who do not have to sell.

I tell these sellers that, first, a quiet listing is impossible; once someone sees the property, the news that it is on the market will be known in hours. The caretaker will tell other caretakers. The maid will tell other maids. Somehow it always filters out.

Second, it is not in their interest to have a quiet listing. I take them back to the goal of all marketing — multiple buyers, not one buyer. I try to focus the seller on why it is so important to include everyone in the sale, have open houses for the brokerage community, do direct mailings, coordinate open houses, etc. All these efforts are to get them to that one point in time of having multiple bidders and to raise the comfort level to bid of the few buyers out there.

> Bad agent rapport undermines the whole effort to control a positive psychology of the sale.

Third, I explain that trying to keep their sale a secret will seem odd to agents and buyers. If you have what constitutes a non-exclusive "open listing" and word gets out that you are showing the house (it will), then agents will think you are refusing to cooperate and trying to do an in-house sale. As a result they will feel shunted and will badmouth the property. Bad agent rapport undermines the whole effort to control a positive psychology of the sale. Thus, "quiet listings" don't please serious agents. They only want to bring their buyers to sellers who want to sell. Quiet listings alienate the very people you are trying to attract.

Fourth, a quiet listing empowers buyers, not sellers. Lacking an organized marketing campaign, the buyers will never feel the threat of competition and the resulting urgency to act we need to create. The "quiet" listing undermines the very reason to act, let alone pay up.

All of this immediately has the effect of tainting the property and the sale and most assuredly results in a lower price for the seller.

Finally, my experience has taught me that when sellers offer a quiet listing, it is likely they have also offered that same listing to half a dozen other agents. Instead of excitement a "quiet listing" leads agents to react to it with a big yawn, dismissing the property: "Oh, they have been trying to quietly sell that for years." It leads to diminishing the status and importance of the property. And, frankly, it does you no good either.

Quiet listings from a marketing point of view usually equate to quiet death. If the sellers still insist, pass on the property.

Preparing Your Seller for Success

Marketing Tools: Professional Photography

Today, professional photography is a necessary tool of serious luxury marketers. (If this is not an issue for you, skip this section and move on.) But if you have ever been tempted to cut corners and utilize your own camera skills, avoid it unless you are a professional.

Photographs are the primary means by which someone views a property before a site visit. You use them in the local and (sometimes) national press, color brochure, MLS, print ads, PR and most importantly, on the Internet. Those photographs largely control everything buyers see, feel, and think about this property. Don't skimp on photos.

Since this is often a costly expenditure, you might ask the seller if they have had any professional photography already done. If so, determine whether it can give the quality result you want.

> The point of the photographs is to get someone to call.

Viewing past photographs of the property can be interesting because it can tell you what the seller thinks is important about the house. These photographs can even be valuable for showing how something used to look, providing a sense of history or nostalgia to a property. Sometimes older shots can be cleverly incorporated into recent photography, making for a more interesting brochure. Finally, the photographer may still be around. Since she already worked for the seller, sometimes you can get better pricing on updated photos.

While good photography is expensive, you can keep costs down in other ways. One is to put a photographer on retainer. Sometimes it's possible to work out an arrangement under which you employ her on a monthly basis in return for priority treatment and reduced fees. It does, however, require volume of listings and therefore is something that should be done by the company or broker/owner or by a consortium of agents who pool their resources and share photographer services. Also, don't underestimate the power of being able to say to your clients that you have on retainer one of the best photographers in the area.

Often there is a lot to photograph—the house atop the hill with its views of the water, the pool, entry gates, the main rooms and guesthouses—all of which can be costly. For urban agents, the costs can sometimes be slightly less because there is less to photograph, but these shots usually require skillful interior lighting that can incur additional costs.

> While photographs should tease the buyer into wanting to know more, they must never be better than the property itself.

Photography should not tell the whole story. The point of the photographs is to get someone to call, to create a mood or emotion that sparks someone's interest.

Every luxury marketer should have a list of photographers used for different jobs. Some are very good at exteriors and getting mood shots with clouds and sun. Others are good with shadows and light and how they fall on the exterior. Some know how to make a lot out of a little; others know how to take a lot and reduce it to only the best shots.

Aerial photography is often a must for larger properties, but be careful of anything other than helicopter shots. Except for the largest ranches, many airplane shots are just too far away, making for granular photographs. Helicopter shots or even cherry picker shots taken from a hoist can give what you want without losing sight of the property itself.

For a sample of spectacular photography, peruse *Architectural Digest* magazine. The artistry of the photography can often convey the beauty of the property. For example, a palatial set table or artfully arranged chair grouping can convey the luxuriousness of the property without full-scale room shots. I always keep a list of *Architectural Digest* photographers that I hired for very special properties where their kind of artistry was needed. Know in advance that this can be expensive.

One way to defray the cost is to ask the sellers if they would like to have a visual remembrance of their property and share in the cost. Many sellers like the idea—for themselves or family members—and will appreciate that they may be getting thousands of dollars worth of professional photographs done for half the price.

Finally, it is important for your clients to know that professional photography should never make the house look better than it actually is.

Instead, photographs should tease the buyer into wanting to know more. Pictures better than the actual property result in the buyer's first emotion being disappointment. That is not how you want a showing to start.

Marketing Tools: Broker Open Houses

Do you view open houses as just a boring necessity to appease homeowners? Have you ever relegated them to marketing assistants or newbie agents who want to help out because they have nothing else to do? If so, this is a mistake.

The purpose of the open house is to begin controlling the psychology of the sale. The goal is not cerebral or informational, e.g., memorizing the square footage or taxes. Rather, it is visceral. Your job is to create a positive buzz that energizes the brokerage community. The open house is the first and the most important way to do it.

A second goal is to give the agents takeaway sound bites to overcome objections raised by buyers. Because I consider the broker open house to be one of the most important events in the whole marketing campaign, I am always there. I stand at the door to greet and to say goodbye. Inside I station other people to answer questions and to support enthusiasm for the sale (enthusiasm, by the way, sells more real estate than information).

It is my job to make sure that when they leave, the agents have the sound bites necessary to sell this property. That means I ask them certain questions, such as, *"What do you think?" "Are there any problems you see?" "What will you say when you present the property to your buyer?"*

If agents occasionally voice negativity about a property, I find that what they are really saying is just a reflection of what they have heard their buyers say during past tours of properties. For this reason, I want them to articulate their objections. I want to hear everything they have to say right at the open house. Once they are known, I can then reflect on those objections, formulate a response, and thereby allow them to feel that I am a source of help and support for dealing with their buyer. If they don't voice their objections to me at the open house, I cannot formulate the necessary responses.

> What they are really saying is just a reflection of what they have heard their buyers say.

Control the psychology of the sale by providing such sound bite answers to objections. Remember: every objection is just something that an agent feels their buyers will say—they really just want an answer from you to help them persuade their buyer. Your job is to help overcome the objection for them, enthusiastically and passionately.

Giving guided tours to small groups of agents is an excellent way to do this. I try to make sure that every group has a guide to take them around, which sometimes requires helpers at the open house. All are coached beforehand on what to say, and each should be thoroughly pumped about the sale. By now it should not be lost on you that if you can get five experienced agents to help you and they are thoroughly briefed and pumped about the listing, you now have five apostles to spread the good news about this property and maybe even sell their own buyers on it.

I also want to avoid agents speeding through the open house because they have so many other properties to see. If possible and if there is any hope of getting a good crowd, I try to schedule the open house on a day when the agents are not on caravan tour with others. Yes, that means that I may not get the property into the market immediately after listing it, but that is fine. Recall, my goal is not to get it into the market quickly if I think I will have only a few buyers. Rather, it is to find the buyers I need to get it sold. If that means waiting to get a larger crowd who can spend more time at the property, so be it. The agents who operate in the market have a 90-95 percent chance or better of having the buyer. I don't want to rush their time at the property or with me. Rather, I want them to spend at least half an hour or longer and take back to their office the excitement about the property generated by myself and my team.

In every brokerage community there is either a buzz around a property that induces agents to sell it or there are doubts that give them second thoughts about showing it. If agents don't like a property for any number of reasons, that dislike has a way of filtering back into the agent pool. Agents who may have never seen the property start to hear negative reports and those reports can take on a life of their own.

> Restricting access to an open house can give the property a negative reputation because it miffs the excluded agents.

After your open house, when agents go back to their office, you want them to say to their colleagues, "You missed a great one today."

The Lingerers

My experience with open houses is that the agents who linger longest have the fewest buyers. And because these agents seem to have extra time on their hands, they are prone to talk, and talk.

Though it can be tiresome and time consuming to talk to them, you should. You want as many voices as possible talking up your listing. By making your open house guests feel like gold, you are recruiting a formidable force to help promote the property. The fact that they are talkers makes them valuable mouthpieces for you in the agent community.

When the Seller Does Not Want an Open House

Many luxury homeowners would rather avoid having an open house. They often view the practice as invasive and a violation of their privacy.

It's important to explain that the open house is meant to create and control a positive view of the property. It is less to convey information than to influence what agents say about the listing and to impart enthusiasm and hear objections. It is part of your controlling the psychology of the sale. We memorized the following script for sellers who did not want an open house.

> *"I know how you must feel. Many of my clients have felt the same way. But what they have found is that having an open house is crucial to controlling the psychology of the sale and actually cuts down on traffic into the property."*

Such a script helps to validate the seller's fears while also demonstrating empathetically that other clients have had the same concerns. Their reconsideration and then consent to an open house helped to keep invasiveness to a minimum but get the property sold.

Open Houses for Neighbors and the Client List

Another important open house is one held for the neighbors and for your client list. It will also be the least attended, so prepare for few people. Nonetheless, abutters and neighbors are some of your best prospects. Not only will the neighbors want to know what is going on with the property, but the buyer may be one of them.

The neighbors should be sent a formal invitation or letter with an RSVP (a telephone call or e-mail also work). Why? Because it is highly likely that few will attend, so you don't want to waste time sitting around waiting. Confirm attendance ahead of time. Your letter might say something like this:

Dear Neighbor:

> *We have been hired by Mr. and Mrs. _____ to market their property at _____. As part of our marketing campaign, we like to make sure the neighborhood is informed of our efforts. Additionally, we like to be able to answer questions.*
>
> *We invite you to a private open house at the property at __ p.m. on such and such a day. This open house is only for area residents and a proprietary list of potential buyers. If you or someone you know would like to attend, please RSVP at 000-222-1111.*
>
> *Please call the same number if you should have any questions about the property or our marketing efforts.*

Sincerely,

David M. Michonski
Marketing Consultant

This invitation provides area residents with a direct line to you, and early access to the property. Know in advance that if neighbors attend, they usually do so because (a) they are nosy, (b) they know a potential buyer, or (c) they're interested in buying it themselves.

> While the neighbors want to know what is going on with the property, they may also provide you with a buyer.

Because the likelihood of getting a crowd is slim and because you want to create an atmosphere of interest in the property, ask the seller if you can supplement the invitation list with a proprietary list of past or current clients and customers. Since these markets are small and people travel in the same circles, it is possible that someone in your client list will know an interested buyer. Private open houses for neighbors and proprietary lists are akin to a yard sign advertising a property "For Sale."

Since there is much curiosity associated with selling a celebrity property, client and neighbor open houses are probably not possible. But when they are, expect a large crowd.

(First Peek) Open Houses for Society Agents

Then there are the society agents. We all know them. They may do only one sale a year, but it is usually a big or prominent one. Real estate for them is a sideline activity, usually done as a favor for friends at the club. To the extent they prospect, it is at the beauty salon, or on the beach at Caneel Bay, or at the Junior League debutante ball.

As a group, however, they sell a good portion of the luxury real estate in upscale communities; therefore, you must make them your allies. This is especially true if you are just breaking into the luxury homes market (see Chapter 12). I like to treat society agents differently from mass market agents by having a special open house for the serious luxury agents together with the society agents. This is usually just a handful of people, rarely more than twenty or thirty. Schedule it just before the mass open house or just afterwards—when it is done is less important than how it is done. I recommend a personal direct call that goes something like this:

> "I have listed _____ and I will be having a private viewing only for a select number of luxury agents. I would like you to be one of them."

If you do serve food at this open house, make it special. A couple of bottles of Champagne and some caviar or *foie gras* on small toast will do the trick, or anything that helps to make attendees feel different from everyone else. You want this group to be allies in controlling what is thought and said about the listing. If you treat mass market agents like gold, treat these agents like platinum.

> If you treat mass market agents like gold, treat these agents like platinum.

On Valuables in Properties at Broker Open Houses

One reason sellers resist an open house is the presence of their valuables. If valuables hinder your ability to sell the property, ask your seller to remove them. The property should not be thought of as Fort Knox. You are trying to sell a piece of real estate, which, when sold, will be emptied of them anyway. If they are not removed, you'll spend more time worrying about the valuables than on generating positive buzz. That, too, defeats the purpose of the open house.

Sometimes your seller insists on keeping art on the property, as was the case with the heirs of a major estate who hired my partner, JoAnne Kennedy, and me to market their ten-room apartment on Gracie Square in Manhattan. Through Christie's auction house, the family was selling the largest collection of contemporary art ever brought to market—worth hundreds of millions of dollars—each piece being worth more than the entire apartment many times over. The property had more than $100 million worth of artwork on just the spiral staircase going to the second floor.

For the agent open house, the family hired several armed guards (uniformed and plainclothes) and we also stationed about a dozen of our own personnel throughout the apartment. We had the open house, artwork and all, and succeeded in selling the apartment.

Public Open Houses

A public open house reduces the prestige of the property. For this reason, I avoid them. There are, however, exceptions, including:

- Vacant properties, usually those owned by builders (most of the showings will be to curiosity seekers rather than serious buyers, but traffic is important here)
- Mature luxury markets like Beverly Hills, Palm Beach, Manhattan and Greenwich, where the traffic coming in is more likely to be able to afford the properties
- A gated community where everyone is screened upon entry

Marketing Tools: Marketing by Arranging Property Tours for Two to Four Listings

In major estate areas, one way to highlight your property among agents is to arrange a property tour of several properties. Three or four is a good number. This is a kind of exclusive agent open house focused on special properties. If yours is clearly the best, you need not worry about being grouped with inferior listings, because the tour allows you to stand out. If you are not the best in the group, then you benefit by being lumped with better properties.

Such an event is also ideal for your clients to attend with you because it allows them to quickly see their competition. Such tours can be important reality checks for clients and serve to help them see first hand what is on the market, especially in down markets.

Marketing Tools: The Uses and Abuses of Color Brochures

Since luxury marketing was started by Previews in 1933, the color brochure has been a staple marketing tool. For more than seventy-five years, consumers have associated the color brochure with luxury marketing.

The original purpose of these brochures was to lure distant buyers with photos and a write-up of the properties' amenities. For instance, Jim Retz, while at Previews, handled the sale of movie and TV icon Dean Martin's home in Hidden Valley, California: a sixty-three-acre estate with a fourteen-room Spanish Colonial residence and a small golf course, helipad, and even bear cages. Upon putting it on the market he invited agents from the entire West Coast. One agent from San Jose took the six-page, four-color brochure to Japan and sold the property to an offshore buyer, literally sight unseen.

Today the Internet has largely supplanted brochures; buyers can now conveniently view multiple pictures and an enormous amount of information about the property online.

Nevertheless, I endorse the color brochure as a necessary cost of luxury marketing. Why?

* *The seller wants one*
  The most important reason is, of course, that it pleases the sellers. They want one and expect one per tradition, so don't start

your relationship arguing over a $500 brochure. If you are going to do it properly, the bulk of the expense will be for professional photography.

- *The Tiffany box effect*
Sometimes how you view something is influenced by how it is wrapped. A beautiful presentation can make a difference. A color brochure sets a property apart and makes it special.

- *It makes the buyer feel good*
Everything we do for buyers in luxury marketing is focused on raising their comfort level to induce them to bid freely, eagerly and aggressively. The color brochure says, "This is no ordinary property. It is a property for someone extraordinary, like me."

- *It is a means of communicating from a distance*
It talks to people from afar in a different way than the Internet; since every property online has six to ten pictures the distinction among properties is blurred. By sending out a brochure to an interested party, you counteract the leveling effect of the Internet by distinguishing your listing from others.

Tool Kit: Color Brochure Mailings

In the fall, when Wall Street investment banks and brokerage firms published their lists of new managing directors or senior vice presidents in the *New York Times* and the *Wall Street Journal,* I would cut out the ad and put those names into a database.

I would also make a copy of the ad and circle the names with a yellow highlighter. The address of the firms was usually printed at the bottom. I then sent each a copy of the ad with his name circled (who doesn't love to be noticed?) and the color brochures for a sampling of our listings, usually with a cover letter that read something like this:

Dear (Rising Star):

Congratulations on your new appointment as Managing Director of _____. Now you deserve something to match your new title and position. Enclosed is a sampling of some of our current inventory. Call me to schedule an appointment.

With hearty congratulations and best wishes for your continued success,

Sincerely,

David M Michonski
David@PowerMarketing.pro
1-662-LUXURY 0 (Direct)

The color brochure allows for this kind of marketing. It is very personal. It is directed at buyers who at some point will want to find a new place that fits their position. But most importantly it sends them a strong message that you are someone who knows how to market. It also tells the seller that you know how to target their property at the right people.

Watch your local papers for all such advertisements in any industry in your area. After all, these people took out an ad to be noticed, so notice them by sending them your brochures.

Timing the Mailing

These "rising stars" will soon be part of the bonus pool in their firms. Once their names were entered into my database, I would contact people at Wall Street firms to find out when bonus day was. Every year I would try to schedule a similar package to arrive within a week of bonuses with a letter something like the following:

Dear _____:

Enclosed are a few things to help you make the most of this year's bonus pool. Call me to arrange an appointment.

Sincerely,

David M. Michonski
David@PowerMarketing.pro
1-662-LUXURY 0 (Direct)

Every year the mailing list would grow and any returns would be culled. My efforts usually resulted in a few new listings every year.

Sellers also loved the mailing and appreciated my pinpoint marketing on their behalf.

A Tool for Other Agents

Since it's likely that the buyer will come from another agent, the color brochure is an ideal tool for them to use with their buyers. We always put our company logo on the back of the brochure instead of the front, so that other agents could staple or paste their card over it. Many brokers, especially smaller ones, as in my Sunninghill Farm example, will put the color brochure in their windows to glamorize them and lead buyers to think that they handle properties like this. Others, like Jim Retz's San Jose selling agent, will take them to show buyers. This is exactly what the brochure is for—to capture buyers' interest.

When another agent puts together a list of properties for a buyer tour, guess which properties stand out in the package? While other homes have MLS sheets for their listing data, you have professional color photographs printed on high quality card stock.

I always made sure that other brokers and their agents were well equipped with color brochures. I sent the brochure, along with other company listings, once a quarter to the brokerage community. It not only provided other agents with a tool to give their buyers, but it helped to set my properties (and me) above the competition. Such mailings almost always resulted in additional showings.

Useful for Listing Appointments

We all know that "a picture is worth a thousand words," and nowhere is that truer than in your listing appointments. I always prominently displayed the color brochure in every listing appointment. At a minimum they made for colorful demonstrations of how many sellers had listed with me or my firm. Easy on the eye, nice to hold, they helped show my range and breadth of properties. A large package of luxury color brochures makes upscale sellers feel they are in the company of success.

Tool Kit: Virtual Tours and Videos

Virtual tours or marketing videos that offer 360-degree views allow someone to get a feel for a home. They provide a sense of walking through a property and a good sense of the grounds. When done well, they can be great sales tools. If you go this route, invest in a good videographer and take care not to show so much of the property that you're no longer teasing and creating interest.

There are several caveats. First, everything I said about photography applies here. Are you any better at making videos than taking pictures? Probably not. Therefore it should be done professionally, which can be expensive.

Lesson: Floor Plans

Floor plans are not appropriate for resale homes. A simple story demonstrates why. Over several months we received about a dozen inquiries for floor plans on various properties that had been advertised in a national publication. All the inquiries came from the same California address. We routinely replied either that the floor plan was not available (which generally it was not) or that it would be made available only to pre-qualified buyers who had seen the property. Even then it would be made available only upon our meeting the buyer and if the seller felt comfortable doing so.

Because all the inquiries came from the same reply address, I grew suspicious and did some research. I learned that the return address was a California state penitentiary.

Tool Kit: Print Advertising

Few things in the real estate brokerage business waste more money than print advertising. In its best days print advertising never produced more than 14 percent of buyers nationally. It was higher in cities that relied on classifieds and where there was no MLS, but still it has always been the industry's most underperforming expenditure.

Worse, it can be every real estate agent's crutch. If advertising could sell property, then sellers would save a lot of money by just hiring an advertising company. Overemphasis on advertising, therefore, is not only a great waste of money, but it, in effect, teaches sellers that all you are is an advertising company. At this point in the book, I think you already know that you are much, much more than that.

What use therefore does print advertising have?

The answer lies in who reads ads even more than consumers. The answer is other agents. Ads serve as a catalyst for other agents to act. Agents see your ad and think to themselves that they had better call their buyer on your property and present it. Ads therefore help focus agents on listings and remind them to call their buyers.

Ads can also help at the beginning of a sale—a time when you want the neighbors or the abutters to be moved to action. Since the beginning of a listing is the time when there is the greatest urgency to act, placing an ad during this initial period may well be the best print ad spend you can make. Another good ad spend is ironically after there is demonstrated interest in a property. Advertising after you found a buyer quickens their interest by creating a threat that the new advertising will produce more buyers. The ad thus creates an urgency to act. Stalled or hesitant buyers (if you tell them or their buyer agents about the upcoming ad) can be moved into acting, too, just by knowing the property will be advertised this weekend.

Finally, ads serve as image creation for you and for your firm. But the question remains, is it worth the cost? That question will have to be settled by you and your firm because it depends on the local market conditions. If you have a serious lifestyle magazine in your market, such as *San Diego, Westport, Greenwich* magazine in Connecticut or *Quest* magazine in Manhattan, which upper-end buyers and sellers are reading, then the expenditures on image advertising may be well worth the price.

If all your competitors are in such magazines, then not being in them can send a negative impression. Image marketing is a form of branding of you or your firm within the upper-end market and should therefore be considered as part of an overall branding campaign. But just putting some properties on a page in your local lifestyle magazine is not going to do it. You need the advice of image consultants for this.

One final example of a useful print ad spend: paid advertising accompanying stories printed about yourself or your listings. This could include taking out advertorial pages in the local lifestyle magazine and then inserting your own collection of luxury listings in that issue. Local lifestyle magazines often have a long shelf life as consumers tend to leave these types of magazines around on their coffee table to read.

Lesson: Business Cards

One of the best things that we ever did within our Previews Program at Coldwell Banker Hunt Kennedy in Manhattan was to spend for business cards and stationery that had a look and feel so upscale that upon handling by consumers the image was set. Our cards were oversized, of thick stock, and felt high quality. They cost about eight times what normal business cards cost.

Our agents reported terrific results from these cards and from the matching stationery. One top agent in our firm, Patrick Lilly, reported getting a multi-million-dollar listing immediately after sending out letters on the new stationery—something he attributed to the upscale feel of the material.

Expenditures for collateral materials of this kind, when part of an overall image program, may contribute even more to setting your image than the expense of running a full page in the local lifestyle magazine.

Tool Box: The Internet

Today the consumer, both million dollar and mass market, is in the same place: on the Internet—whether it is Wall Street investment bankers who are surfing www.Realtor.com on their lunch hour or couples going online after putting the kids to bed. The consumer no longer takes several days off to meet an agent, get in a car, and start scurrying around neighborhoods to find a home.

Consumers today in effect pre-qualify properties via the photos, virtual tours, and even urban and new home floor plans found on real estate listing websites.

Given your desire for the widest and broadest exposure possible, this means properties must be on as many sites as possible. At my firm we put our listings on no fewer than seventy-three websites. Websites

> Get the net out there and make sure it is in the largest body of water with the most fish swimming in it.

come and go and whatever I might list here will be outdated by the time this is published. But the Internet is here to stay. The Internet, not specific websites, is the magic bullet.

Like most firms, we built our own website but the problem—as with all websites—is that once built, traffic has to get there. Isn't it best just to put your clients where the traffic already is? Putting our listings on those seventy-three websites did just that.

My advice: throw the net for the fish as far and as wide and with as large a net as you can, but get the net out there and make sure it is in the largest body of water with the most fish swimming in it.

Marketing Tools: International

Most agents today want the ability to get their listings in front of targeted foreign audiences. As of this writing, international sites offer precious little ability (if any) to get your listings directly in front of consumers in foreign countries.

While there have been many attempts to create an international MLS, all have confronted the reality that co-brokering listings is simply not that common in countries outside the United States. Even where there are mature markets like Ireland and England, the emphasis is on smaller commissions and selling a property directly oneself. The 5 percent to 6 percent commission that prevails throughout most of the United States is rarely found elsewhere. As a result, there is less incentive to offer co-brokerage to others or to pay a referral fee. This hinders the ability to create the commission-sharing arrangements at the heart of an international MLS.

While the superstructure for making international referrals is in place via the International Consortium of Real Estate Associations (ICREA, founded in 2000) the same lack of a commission high enough to make a referral worthwhile hinders business flow and reduces the usefulness of what could be a dynamic platform. But in the United States, there is still enough of a commission paid by consumers to allow American agents to pay referral fees to non-American agents, which should keep a stream of referrals coming this way, at least for now.

ICREA's website, *www.worldproperties.com* currently has some 3 million listings in thirty countries, but the site is not well marketed to consumers on an international basis. Nonetheless, it certainly does not hurt you and can be reassuring to your clients if you inform them that their property can be found there.

Even the major franchises have had their share of challenges. Language and translation issues, as well as measurement issues for international listings, have been challenges for American-centric franchise sites. While the major franchises, especially Sotheby's International Realty, have the ability to get a listing in front of an affluent international audience, there is still very limited opportunity to get all listings in front of a whole country and engage in the kind of exposure that unleashes a competitive urgency to act—the key to *power marketing.*

> www.worldproperties.com currently has some 3 million listings in thirty countries.

But because international marketing of residential real estate is such an emerging field, I have decided to team up with a former colleague from the National Association of Realtors® to write a book on marketing homes worldwide. It should be on www.amazon.com and my own website by the summer of 2012 and is titled *Global Connections: Marketing Homes Internationally.*

Marketing Tools: Direct Mail

Earlier I mentioned a direct mail piece that I had done for Wall Street bankers and the elite of major investment firms. Such direct mail pieces should be replicated for whatever industry is the dominant player in your market—the auto industry in Gross Pointe or Silicon Valley in San Francisco, for example.

Wherever you operate, you should also have a list of the owners of the properties that make up your market, and they should be direct mailed your listings. This puts your listings in front of the very audience that is likely to buy them or that may know someone who will. Such a direct mail piece means that when it comes time for them to list their home, yours will be the name that comes into their mind. Sending at least a sampling of your brochures to this audience on a regular (quarterly) basis should be a staple of your marketing efforts.

Marketing Tools: E-Blasts

As I indicated earlier, because there is a more than 90 percent chance that the buyer will come through the brokerage community it is your most important target audience. Today, while beautiful color brochures on thick stock still make an impression that is worth the cost for all the benefits I have articulated, e-blasts are a less expensive way to keep properties in front of the local (and non-local) brokerage community and to provide regular updates on the status of your listings. Once the list is set up (which may take some time), you can communicate with this group on short notice. When you are engaged in serious negotiations with several buyers, e-blasts are excellent ways to communicate that there is serious activity on a property and that if anyone has buyers, they should bring them now or forever hold their peace.

Tool Box: Just Listed and Just Sold Cards

I have touted direct mail largely for image enhancement, but it can also help with finding a buyer. By far the most successful direct mail piece is a Just Listed or Just Sold card. These should convey the upscale image you are seeking. Getting them in front of your direct mail list of luxury homeowners is a great example of drip marketing. For homeowners to get a Just Listed card one week and then another several weeks later, followed by a Just Sold, and more each month thereafter, is not only to keep them informed that the market is moving, but more importantly, that you are moving the market. Well worth the postage.

Marketing Tools: Exposition Marketing and Trade Shows

A related form of marketing by association is the growing number of new expositions to market real estate. In Spain there is the SIMA exhibition that is by far the largest in Europe. In Cannes, France, there is the MIPIM show annually. London has its "American Real Estate Show" that has been held on and off for twenty years. Other such shows are always springing up.

At the NAR annual convention, there is now a growing international property showcase, which thousands of people attend. In effect, you can bring your listings to a world real estate audience once a year at the NAR convention. The International Real Estate Federation, known as FIABCI, has been holding its World Congress for over fifty years and many would-be luxury marketers have attended these shows thinking they might find buyers for their listings.

MARKETING BY ASSOCIATION

Earlier I mentioned bundling your luxury listings with other luxury properties into a broker tour. Marketing the property by association with other upscale products is a way to call attention to the property and comfort buyers that your listing is associated with other comparable luxury products, brands, and events.

- Have an important artist or prestigious art gallery hold a "by invitation only" opening for their artwork in the property.

- Sponsor a trunk show of Gucci or Armani boutique designer-type clothes that bring in highly upscale buyers.

- Allow a charity event that attracts high-end clientele.

- Schedule an antique car show to be held on the grounds of the estate.

- Host an antique boat show, if it is a waterfront property with sufficient dockage or mooring area available

Is it worth attending any of these? Going to NAR is always worthwhile, but if results are measured in finding a buyer and selling a listing, then the answer for the rest is usually no.

You may, however, wish to attend these shows for the sake of traveling abroad and trying to make it tax deductible. If so, they have value. Also, mentally, such expositions are always broadening experiences that get you out of your comfort zone. That may have value. Traveling to make new relationships can be fun, too. At the same time such travel can distract you from the urgent business of staying focused on prospecting and marketing to the audience where the buyer is actually lurking, with the agents in your market.

Marketing Tools: Charity Events and Charity Programs

Better to do charity work out of a sincere belief in the work being done —not for business purposes. Being part of charities and on committees can be excellent business-building venues, but don't engage in them for that purpose. Let whatever business relationships come out of it be welcome byproducts, not the reason for supporting the charity.

Charity events, however, can be a form of marketing by association. If the seller is receptive to the possibility of opening her home (I suggest "by invitation only") to a charity group, this can be an effective way to drive traffic. But it should be a high-end charity that gets quality traffic walking through the property.

Marketing Tools: Publicity Before and After the Sale

Before the Sale

Publicity on a property before the sale depends on two things: the seller's permission and your creativity. Such publicity is gold if you can get it. Why? Because it sets your property apart and gives it a little celebrity value (whether it deserves it or not), and it increases the buyers' comfort level with the property. Let's deal with the two variables.

Your seller must first consent to publicity and many sellers do not want it. Many do not even want it known that they are selling, let alone having such news splashed across the media. You are forced to respect that. However, if you are dealing with a celebrity property, or a property that is going to get media attention anyway (it may have some renown, may have been the site for a movie shoot, or may have some local historical value), you should inform your seller in advance that media attention, however unwanted, will arrive. You need to prepare him for it. If the seller is shy, he needs to know in advance that he is going to be in the public eye. But especially if he dislikes media attention, he needs to know that you have not caused the publicity. Rather, you want to be the person who forewarned him and who will try to handle it.

Sometimes you can preempt media attention by doing something quite counterintuitive, such as issuing a press release and even holding a press conference. You can thus influence what is being said, for example, by suggesting alternate stories or points of interest about the property, different from what the media will accentuate. If you know what they will likely say and there is nothing you can do about it, you can and should probably say nothing. All this is defensive action.

On the other hand, if your seller does not mind some media attention or actually encourages it, you should engage in proactive promotion to get the property out there. Often this is pretty mundane stuff such as:

> *123 Jackson Road came on the market this week at a price of $9.2M. The property, formerly the home of our town founders, is now owned by Mr. and Mrs. Kendal Rogers, who descended from town founder, Ermile Jackson. The sale is being handled by Ken Smith of Famous Properties.*

That is it. Sometimes by just giving the facts straightaway, you avoid all the unwanted baggage that can get added to a story.

If your seller wants publicity but there is not much to say about the property, get creative. You have to find something that would lend itself to a story. Usually this can revolve around the owners, for example:

> *Such and such estate is the home of _____, who was one of the owners of...*

Stories can also revolve around architecture, history, size, or unusual events that occurred. You will need to sit down with the seller and try to figure out an angle to use in promoting the property via public relations.

Hiring a professional is often the way to go, especially if you are not good at handling the press. Make the recommendation to the seller that, given the circumstances, an outside third party professional should handle it.

This is an expense that you should not pick up. After all, the publicity is a consequence of who the seller is or the property the seller owns. The publicity is likely to rebound to the seller's benefit or controlling it will protect the seller. Either way, it should be his cost and you should coordinate with the PR people, not pay them.

If the seller is a celebrity, they will likely have a publicist and you need to sit down with them to know the storyline in advance and how you are going to react to questions.

After the Sale

Publicity after the sale should not be about your success. Remember that even though you orchestrated it all, the sale is not your event. It is a private business transaction between a seller and a buyer to which you are privileged. In addition, the respective parties may have individuals whom they want to protect from the press—children, relatives, friends, employers, or employees. Or they may not want those around them to know about the transaction. It is your job to protect those concerns as much as possible.

Remember that every sale should be worth at least five referrals and if you succeed in alienating the seller after the sale, you will not likely get those referrals and their inherent business-building opportunities.

> Even though you orchestrated it all, the sale that just occurred is not your event.

Indeed, the seller may never talk with you again and may even turn on you and become a mouthpiece of bad press.

If the parties want publicity and you are allowed to say something, what should you say?

The press will likely want to know the price so forewarn your seller that it will be disclosed. It is public information and will get out eventually, so why not control it yourself? The press will also want to know who the buyer is. If you try to hide it, it can generate intense media attention that may be the opposite of what you want. Better to just tell them and get it over with.

Finally, the press will want to know what the buyer is going to do with the property. You can dismiss this line of questions by simply saying, "That has not been determined" or "We don't know" or "We have no comment on that."

How to "Blow Your Own Horn" (Discreetly)

The obvious fact is that after a major or high-profile sale, you want to get more business and build upon the sale for the next listing. While this involves restraining yourself, here's what I have found works best.

I suggest reserving comment about the sale from the mass market and, if possible, mentioning it only when trying to list a new property in the privacy of a prospective client's living room. Arm yourself with plenty of color brochures of the property with "SOLD" stickers across the top, and talk about the sale in this non-public setting. Here you can tell the news at the exact time you want it known—when trying to list a new property.

> It arrives via word of mouth from other influential people—by far the best type of publicity for which you could hope.

If the sales mentioned in your listing pitch are significant ones, expect that the potential new clients will announce to their friends that they have just hired the agent who handled the sale of such and such. In this way the message gets to exactly the upscale market you want to reach, except it arrives via word of mouth from other influential people —by far the best type of publicity for which you could hope.

case study ▼▼▼

Selling His Honor, the Mayor

One of our agents in Manhattan, Lucy Martin Gianino, and my partner, JoAnne Kennedy, handled the purchase by Rudolph Giuliani, then mayor of New York, and his wife, Judith Nathan Levine, of their apartment on the Upper East Side of Manhattan. Could a New York real estate agent ask for a more high-profile customer than His Honor, the mayor? Obviously, this was a top-secret transaction. One can easily imagine the lengths to which Lucy and JoAnne went to shuttle the mayor in and out of buildings without creating a media event.

"No publicity" was the ground rule set by the mayor, and for years JoAnne and Lucy were unable to get credit in the press for securing the trust of one of the most famous men in the world. Nonetheless, at the closing JoAnne made sure to bring a camera and succeeded in getting a picture of herself with the mayor, his wife, and Lucy.

That picture proudly went into most listing presentations and stood on JoAnne's desk next to a picture of her, former Mayor Ed Koch, and me having lunch together.

The placement of the pictures was no accident and anyone sitting in front of JoAnne's desk could not help but see her with two of the most famous, powerful, and influential men in New York City...and get the message. When we had receptions or meetings in our offices with sellers and their intermediaries (lawyers, accountants, trust officers), those two pictures made the point at the appropriate time and to the appropriate people.

▲ ▲ ▲

Marketing Tools: Making the Last Call to Get Buyers

Throughout this book I have emphasized "the last call" as one of the most powerful marketing actions you can perform to create an urgency to act while controlling the psychology of the sale.

We can all recall being at an auction when the gavel is about to come down and remembering what can occur when everyone has one last chance to bid. This is the tool that gets your clients the highest price possible—sometimes a record price. But it also belongs in this chapter because it is one of the finest tools you have to find additional buyers and get them to your listings. How?

When you make the last call to agents who have shown a property, here is what happens.

- They tell the agents sitting next to them that there is a lot of action on your property.

- You give the agents you called a reason to call their buyers.

- The agents sitting around the one you called are reminded to show the property to their buyers.

- Those who have already seen the property and passed on it decide that, given the action, maybe they should give it another peek.

- The agents you called have additional buyers now and think to show your property.

Making the last call also means calling the property's neighbors and abutters again. After all, they have been living next door to the property for years. The complacency of being unable to imagine someone else living there needs to be broken by your last call. This is the final chance for them to step up and buy it. If they are ever to act, they need the last call.

Luxury Property Marketing Requires More Qualification of Buyers than Ordinary Marketing

While you should welcome and encourage all agents to bring their buyers to your listing, you should not confuse that action with allowing just anyone to view a property. Just because you make an offer of cooperation and compensation to other agents and are prepared to include them in your sale does not mean their buyers are qualified.

In luxury real estate you will have to spend more time qualifying the pool of buyers and separating out those who can afford to buy from those who cannot. That takes more time and effort than putting a key box on a listing and letting co-brokers bring anyone and everyone into it.

Such qualifying is your job. It is not up to the selling or co-brokering agents to qualify their customers for you (although they should do so not to waste their own time). Rather, it is emphatically the listing agent's job to qualify everyone. Your sellers expect it. Your fiduciary duty to them demands it. After all, your sellers have artwork, antiques, and other important objects in their homes. You should not be the unwitting conduit for unqualified traffic into their home. Even forgetting the antiques and artwork and valuables, just knowing the layout of a home can provide thieves with enough to return to the property at a later time.

Types of Buyers: "Location Specific" versus "Property Specific"

Before you qualify someone it is helpful to try to categorize them for the type of buyer they are. I like to make a distinction between what I call "location specific" and "property specific" buyers.

Most buyers are "location specific." They want to be in this town and this area and then within a specific price range. They may like one house style over another but generally they will first indicate their price range and location and see what is on the market in that area.

On the other hand, a "property specific" buyer does not care where the property is located as long as it has certain characteristics. This may mean having an in-law suite or accommodation for a ninety-two-foot yacht. She may be searching for a 5,000- to 100,000-acre ranch and not care whether it is in Montana, Wyoming, or Colorado. Or, she may be interested only in mountain or ocean views or insist on being right on a lake, wherever that lake might be. This is a "property specific" buyer.

Therefore, begin by asking whether they are "property specific" or "location specific."

- Ask the agents or the buyers what else they have seen.
- What did they like or dislike about each property?
- Why did they not buy it? (The answer will often give a very good idea of their interest level.)
- How long have they been looking?
- What is their timetable for purchase?

Location Specific vs. Property Specific Buyers

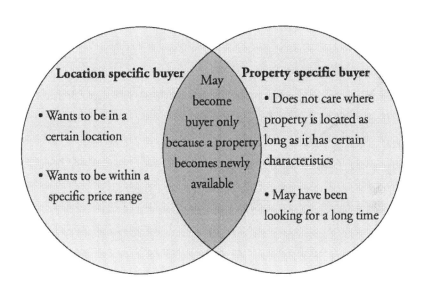

Be aware that the "property specific" buyer may have been looking for a long time. In their case, the length of time looking is not always an indication of a lack of urgency to buy. The property they are seeking could be in any number of locations, and it just takes time to check out such a wide part of the market. Be warned that if they are "one buyer in a million," meaning they are looking for something highly specific, they will know how specialized their interest is and how few others share it. They will need, therefore, a reason to pay up. Given what you have read thus far, you now know what that reason is: credible and defensible value clearly demonstrated and competition or the threat thereof.

Sometimes you learn that a buyer is new in the market and may not have seen much, if anything. Nonetheless, she has become a buyer because a special property now is available. This can be a very good buyer who may be less cognizant of her singularity and therefore more concerned about real or threatened competition and be willing to pay up, making her more motivated.

Qualifying also includes qualifying the agent who is representing the buyer. I like to know how long the agent has known the buyer and how long they have worked together. The amount of time invested gives me an indication of how serious the agent thinks this buyer is and whether the agent feels the buyer is worth the time. There is certainly a code of honor among luxury agents that I believe works well. When you know the agent, you can ask candidly, "Are these people serious?" Ask as many questions as you can, and let the agent explain why the buyer is worth the time.

How, then, do we qualify buyers?

- Ask their financial advisers, banker, lawyer
- Get references
- Call their company
- Check their website or Google them
- Use social networks such as Linkedin or Facebook.

Even though wealthy people are notorious about their desire for privacy, I make it clear that my seller will not allow a showing without strict financial qualification. Therefore, either I must know who the person is or I must know, for example, that she currently lives in, say, an $11M house or is likely to be able to afford this one. Call her company, advisers, and intermediaries as I did with the buyer for Sunninghill to confirm she is who she says. If the individual is part of a public company, go to her website and get her latest annual reports.

Today, information is more public than ever before and easier to get. Indeed, today the issue is when there is no public information about someone. That is a red flag. Under such circumstances it is fine to go back to the buyer and ask for background information to give to the seller. If he is unwilling to provide it, you need to ask for some references. If you cannot get those, beware.

The Problem of International Buyers

Confidentiality issues multiply in the case of foreign buyers. In some cultures, hiding wealth is an ever-present passion; in others, it is considered vulgar to talk about it or display it too garishly. All international buyers feel that by giving up their financial information they are also giving up key negotiating information, and are reluctant to do it.

With such international buyers insist that you cannot show a property unless they are pre-qualified. While you may not be able to get financial information on the foreign purchaser, you can at least get references. None is more critical than their banker. Any foreign buyer must have a banker here in the United States who will handle their fund transfers. If they do not have one yet, then they are not ready to buy. They should have a good immigration attorney, too, for all of the residency issues surrounding a foreign purchase. If they do not have that, they also are not ready to buy.

Be prepared to ask these questions of foreign buyers:

- *"Have you ever bought in the United States? If so, where?"*
- *"Why are you looking to make this purchase?"*
- *"What is your timetable?"*
- *"How long have you been looking?"*

Many such questions, however, will need to be asked obliquely rather than directly; this is an art form in itself, beyond the scope of this book.[19]

With foreign purchasers it is often less security issues that you need to worry about as much as having your time wasted. If you are told that they must see the property by such and such a time because they are leaving the country, you are probably not going to make a sale, unless the property has just come on. If they have been here for a week and they call on the last day, that probably means they are tired of being a tourist and have decided to go see some nice real estate. You don't want to play into that game.

The Takeaway _____

🎩 Other agents are the most vital, powerful, and indispensable marketing tool in your arsenal, because more than 90 percent of the time, they have the buyers.

🎩 Your solid relationship with the agent community is one of the most important reasons a client should hire you. Get testimonials to your reputation from other agents.

🎩 Agent open houses should be used to positively affect the psychology of a sale from the very start and control it along the way.

🎩 Photography must always be high quality, designed to interest and lure, but never tell the whole story or look better than the property itself.

🎩 Arranging a multi-listing (two to four) agent tour may yield buyers, position your property favorably, and serve as a reality check for your homeowners.

🎩 Expose listings on as many high-traffic websites as possible.

🎩 Utilize email blasts for low-cost exposure to agents and to provide "last call" updates.

🎩 Utilize quality marketing materials such as color brochures and high-quality business cards and stationery to enhance your image and that of the property you represent.

🎩 Direct mail pieces (personal letters at bonus time and Just Listed and Just Sold cards) are ideal for targeting an audience, and demonstrating that the market is moving and that you are moving the market.

🎩 Advertising's primary value is as your image builder. It is most effective to force action right at the beginning of a listing or *after* you have found a buyer.

- Market the property in association with high-end events such as charities, but join charities for their own sake, not for business.

- PR is highly effective if your client wants it; when they have no choice, tell the media the name of the seller, the price it sold for, and what the buyer will do with the property.

- Categorize buyers as "property specific" or "location specific."

- Qualify buyers, through their bankers, lawyers, investment advisers, other intermediaries, and reputable agents.

- The international market is still emerging and difficult to access. If you choose to participate, qualify buyers as you would U.S. buyers, also making sure they have their banking and immigration advisers in place.

7

Listings that Explain It All:
Le Domaine Résistance

It's story time. "Le Domaine Résistance" is a fictitious name for a real property and a real story. I have changed the names of those involved to keep our focus on the marketing principles and the lessons to be learned, and away from the characters and personalities.

At first, I thought this story might need updating because the property sale and the saga that accompanied it are old, and the price point, while clearly luxury property at the time, has less relevance for today's pricier market. But the lesson and the instruction it provides withstand time because its challenge, a stale real estate listing, is so relevant to every real estate agent's experiences. The solution clearly summarizes and crystallizes the core principles of *power marketing*.

How do you sell a magnificent luxury estate that has been on the market for eight years and hasn't sold? This answer has everything to do with luxury *power marketing*.

By now you know that the luxury markets are small. Consumers hire you to create and orchestrate competition within these very small markets by employing all the tools discussed in previous chapters. *Le Domaine Résistance* is an excellent example because the primary tool used to create competition and raise buyer comfort levels was nothing more exotic than the tool available to all agents, the Multiple Listing Service to which you belong (although we surely gave the property much broader reach).

My goal: create a market for a property that had been entombed in the market's and the agents' ennui.

How? By orchestrating everyone's comfort level to act, which resuscitated excitement and unfroze local buyers.

Once I created a market that previously did not exist, the property sold for full price.

Another Comment About the MLS

While under attack from all fronts, the Multiple Listing Service system in the United States remains the envy of the world. This system has created the most liquid, efficient, and transparent real estate market anywhere (to appreciate it, just go overseas and try to buy or sell a property.) Because it quickly helps to determine the market for most properties, consumers benefit from it enormously. But very often, for a few simple reasons, the MLS does not work as well at the luxury end of the market.

Markets are pyramids, and at the upper price points, there are fewer potential buyers. Because these buyers do not have to buy, they have little urgency to act. They also know there are not many others in their price category. They know about the lack of liquidity found here. As a result, it is possible that a luxury property may actually have no market when it is listed because the three or four buyers who might be interested are out skiing in Vail, or at their home in the south of France, or do not want to be bothered with looking during the holiday season, or for an infinite number of others reasons they are just not "in the market" when you are bringing a new listing to it.

Thus, at the luxury end you do not get the instant feedback from the market created by the MLS. It is why you and your clients may feel frustrated that you are not getting enough action. It is why your client often may look to you to do something beyond just putting it on the MLS. This often results in a demand to go out and find that "one buyer in a million." Your seller wants a kind of pinpoint marketing and expects you to target the right buyer and to do it now.

To satisfy this request, you may be tempted to perform extraordinary and unnecessary acts, like get on a plane to take your property listing to a foreign buyer—an Arab sheik or a Russian billionaire. But these requests are simply consumers recognizing the limitations of their local market and crying out for agents to do something to create a market for their property.

Enter the case of *Le Domaine Résistance* in Locust Valley, Long Island, New York.

Stepladder Marketing: Creating a Market by Raising Comfort Levels

This is a story about creating a market where the existing market for a particular property is frozen. It is not about getting on a plane and peddling the property in Hong Kong, and it is not about expensive and fancy marketing. It is about orchestrating local agents and local buyers all of whom came through the MLS. Indeed, for this rookie marketer it was my first real luxury listing. From its story I learned the core principles of this book.

The North Shore Gold Mine

The story begins with my former firm, LandVest of Boston, desiring to expand beyond its New England borders. We specialized in only million-dollar-and-up properties that had some uniqueness, often including a large land component. Believing that "under all is the land," we viewed the land (or location) as the key value in most properties, to which we added the improvements. It should not be surprising that all our valuations determined the core land value first.

My senior management looked at the North Shore of Long Island like miners, eyes popping, staring at a vein of gold. Here was one of the greatest collections of estate properties in the world. Here were not just scattered million-dollar mansions, but rather mile after mile of some of the most magnificent estates that had ever been built.

Here the barons of finance like J. P. Morgan and his partner Henry P. Davison created waterfront estates of breathtaking proportions and beauty. The Luckenback and Pratt families built country manors for their families. The Woolworths, Phipps, Whitneys, and other titans of Wall Street all came to be a part of a Great Gatsby scene that is still astonishing today. Here is a staggering collection of landed estate properties: Locust Valley, Mill Neck, Center Island, Brookville, Upper Brookville, Muttontown, Cold Spring Harbor, and then to the west: Roslyn, Manhasset, and even farther west to Kings Point on Great Neck. LandVest wanted in.

Because my wife's family roots were in one of these great estates, I was given the North Shore territory and told to develop it. Of course it was only a small inconvenience that I did not live there, that I had never sold any property there, that a national competitor had established dominant market share already, and that no one had ever heard of my firm, LandVest. It was only a little more mildly inconvenient that I did not know how to get around the North Shore, especially since I lived five hours away in Boston. Nonetheless, my senior management decided that we were going to take the North Shore and our goal was to get the number one market share.

One of the great things about being young is that you can accomplish things because you just don't know any better. That was certainly the case when I, with my very able senior partner, Robert R. Borden III, headed for Long Island.

Bob was of the right Boston lineage, with select boarding school ties, a Social Register listing, and the proper "III" after his name. These attributes helped to allay any suspicion that we LandVest boys were not up to snuff, especially me, the young kid with the name ending in a vowel who grew up in a small mill town in Western Massachusetts. To say I came from the wrong side of the tracks was inaccurate; in my town both sides of the tracks were poor.

Soon we got into our roles: I would be the aggressive, brash young marketer while Bob was the elder statesman, always there in the background, offering wisdom and guidance. We would joke that sellers could be reassured that if I got out of hand Bob would look up from the Social Register in time to see that the situation was corrected quickly and discreetly.

Needing and Getting a Listing

As with all brokers trying to establish themselves, we needed something to sell—a listing that would qualify for our "greater than local exposure." We accomplished that through a brilliant affiliate system created by my colleague John Coburn, Jr. John was a Harvard-educated Bostonian and someone who loved solving problems, and always did. In our case, John took the 10 percent commission we charged and broke it up in a way that a local broker had every incentive to bring to us multi-million-dollar listings and cooperate with us to get them sold.

Here is how it worked. If a local agent had a $3M listing on which he might be able to get a 5 percent or 6 percent commission, he was encouraged to offer the seller yet another alternative. This was to consider putting the property into the LandVest Marketing program. In this case the consumer paid us a 10 percent commission, which we split. Three percent went to the agent who brought us the listing and showed the property for us, 3 percent went to the agent who produced the buyer, and 4 percent went to LandVest to cover our marketing costs and pay our overhead and salaries.

> We got paid more to do everything in this book.

The reason sellers would list with us and pay a higher commission was that we brought greater than local exposure, focus, and a luxury marketing expertise that had resulted in a track record of selling 93 percent of our listings, many at record prices. In other words, they paid us more to do everything I have written about in this book. That 93 percent track record of success easily justified paying us more, especially after they had tried the local markets for six months with no success.

For the local agents who were our scouts for listing opportunities, it meant that they would get no less a commission than they would get normally. Coburn's ingenious system was perfect for local brokers because they had nothing to lose. If they brought us the listing, and we listed it, but they found the buyer, they would get the 3 percent selling fee in addition to the 3 percent showing fee. Thus, they got the same 6 percent commission they might have gotten without us, but now with no cost or risk to them.

As a result, not only was there no disadvantage to introducing us to their sellers, there was a great advantage. We would only accept a listing for a minimum of one year and often for two years, which meant they could control the property for a longer period. Sometimes we would take an up-front fee to cover marketing, but most of the time we fronted the risk of advertising and marketing, something from which the local agents and their managers were happy to have been freed. Perhaps most importantly, they had partners who were experts at getting such major properties sold. It was win-win for all concerned.

A Chance to Break In

Almost as an extra dividend, most local agents also found our system a great way to break into the luxury market simply by bringing us leads and arranging appointments for us. If they could get us in the door, a listing that the local agents might not have been able to get on their own might now be within their grasp. If the homeowner turned us down, the local agent risked nothing because in rejecting us as an alternative marketing vehicle, the client could still list with them locally. In fact, the 10 percent commission we charged made the local commission look like a bargain.

Thus, it was not surprising that when I was invited to address the Douglas Elliman sales meeting in their Locust Valley office one Tuesday, the able manager, Louise O'Rourke, introduced me enthusiastically as a new resource for properties over $1.5M (today it would be over $4M). The manager told the agents that now when they had a lead, they could bring me in on their most challenging properties to see what we could do.

> "You see, David, no one can sell *Le Domaine Résistance*."

One agent, Helen Woodbridge, jumped up with great enthusiasm and yelled across the sales meeting: "I have just the perfect property."[20] Louise asked which one. Helen smiled and said, "*Le Domaine Résistance*, of course." Everyone in the room laughed and applauded Helen for her suggestion. The many nodding heads seemed to approve that this was, indeed, a listing on which I could cut my teeth.

When I asked why they thought it was such a good listing, I learned that the property had been listed for eight years. There was great laughter. Helen ran into her office and produced the original listing form.

"You see, David, no one can sell *Le Domaine Résistance*." Every firm in town had been given the listing at one time or another but never to any avail and now, given the length of time it had been on the market, *Le Domaine Résistance* gave new meaning to the term "a stale property."

The room of agents were utterly delighted by Helen's suggestion. Their facial expressions and body language said, "Yeah, give him that listing. That'll test his skills. We'll be able to see how good he is."

Or as one broker said, "If you can sell that property, you can sell anything."

Indeed. If one were seeking to establish a reputation with a splash, here was the chance of a lifetime. If I could sell this property, I would succeed in planting our flag firmly on the North Shore.

I loved the challenge. So did G. Wade Staniar, our Senior Vice President, fellow Colgate grad, and the person whom I have acknowledged at the beginning of this book as my mentor. Wade loved challenges and supported in full my taking this assignment. So did my boss, Bob Borden.

Having the Right Look

Before I accepted this challenge I asked to see a picture of the property. When I saw it I got excited. *Le Domaine Résistance* had an imposing gate attached to square brick pillars, flanked by two gate houses. Once through the gate, a winding drive went up a gentle hill that sheltered the house from the main road and ended in a courtyard. The house was a whimsical French Normandy design with some Tudor influences, which included turrets and lovely ivy growing up the sides. It was clearly a magnificent estate, what we called a "signature" or "statement" property. No one could possibly drive into this estate and not be impressed even before the main door was opened.

"If you can sell that property, you can sell anything."

Instantly, I accepted the challenge. It had the look, the privacy, the presence that made for setting the image we wanted. It also had the notorious reputation that made the whole project even more exciting. If I could get this one sold, I confidently believed, my competition would wither. A listing that had been on the market for eight years without any offers was the perfect listing with which to start a luxury marketing career.

Helen arranged for a meeting with the seller, who, to my delight, was utterly gracious and charming and more than willing to listen to what I had to say. I got a little more history upon arrival.

The Provenance

Le Domaine Résistance was built in 1913 and expanded by its second owner to include an indoor swimming pool and expansive master

bedroom suite with a private circular staircase descending down a turret to the pool. Isolated behind a red-brick wall and imposing iron gates
and amidst towering tulip trees, the mansion had thirty rooms, fifteen
fireplaces, paneling from England, hand-hewn beams, and *Palais de
Versailles* floors.

The meeting went well and we listed the property. The listing price
was $995,000, $200,000 below our minimum listing at the time (adjusted
for values today it would be over $4M), but it did not matter. The prop-
erty had all the elements needed for a first listing.

One thing to note. The listing agreement stated clearly that we were
authorized to sell the property for $995,000 cash, and it also stated that
if we provided a full price offer with no financing contingency and a
thirty-to-sixty-day closing, we would earn our commission. The seller
did not have to sell, but we had to be paid. We did this on Wade, my
senior partner's, suggestion because a seller who had a property on the
market for so long might just want to change her mind and up the price
if we got near enough to it. We took a one-year listing at 10 percent
commission with no up-front fee. The listing created a beachhead for us
on the North Shore.

The first thing we did was have it photographed to create a stunning color four-page brochure. It was more than what was needed for
a property that did not even meet our minimum listing price, but we
viewed the brochure as something to get attention and make our splash
in the market.

The brochure was mailed out with an announcement to the brokerage community inviting their cooperation in the sale and offering a
3 percent selling fee to anyone with a buyer.

Getting the Inside Scoop

I received dozens of calls from agents. Some wanted to know who
we were and what we were doing in their market. Others called to
inform me of the property's sorry listing history. Others called to
tell me there had never been an offer because the property needed
$500,000 of work. Someone else called to say it needed $700,000 of
work, and another agent estimated the work at around $1M. Still
others called to say we were wasting our time and the seller was not
serious.

This feedback made my two initial jobs clear. The first was to change the psychology of this listing from that of an unsalable property to one firmly centered on the belief that it would be sold. I had to overcome the belief of too many agents that it was a waste of their time because any seller who would allow her property to be on the market for eight years could not possibly be serious.

> I had to overcome the belief of too many agents that it was a waste of their time.

The second job was to get some accuracy on how much work the place needed, knowing that every buyer would exaggerate any work needed and use it as leverage for getting a lower price. It became clear that over the years the issue had escalated with buyers throwing out numbers that were repeated by unknowing agents. What I knew was that whenever we had a wild spread of numbers such as $500,000 to $1M, greater accuracy was required.

To control the psychology of the sale, we had to get it to a place where agents knew what repairs would cost and were convinced that there was hope for a deal.

Estimating the Cost of Work to Be Done

I worked closely with Helen Woodbridge to bring a small army of contractors into the property. There was some pointing necessary on the exterior brick. The driveway needed some patching and new pebbles laid down. One of the brick perimeter walls had cracked and was leaning. The paint on the gates was peeling. Several fieldstones around the pool were cracked. Inside, the parquet floors needed refinishing, and two rooms could have used some re-plastering and repainting where a prior leak had bubbled and stained the wall. The kitchen needed updating and the addition of modern appliances. Door handles needed tightening or outright replacement. The circular stairs in the turret creaked.

Every repair was documented with written estimates. If I thought they were too high, we got a second or a third opinion. At the end of a process lasting about two weeks, I sat down with my client and presented a list. I informed her that the extent of the repairs had become an issue that was affecting the reputation of the property and that we had to bring clarity and accuracy to the discussion. She was delighted that I had taken the time to quantify the work being done, but when presented with the $125,000 to $150,000 price estimate to get it all done, she politely refused to do any of it.

I was disappointed that she would not even consider doing the two least expensive and most impressionable repairs, scraping and repainting the front entry gates and re-plastering and repainting the wall plaster.

But I had to sell this property. At least now we had quantified the amount of repairs and could use written estimates that would help put the seller in a stronger position to counteract the negotiating leverage buyers had been given. At least we knew the repairs were nowhere near the $500,000 to $1M that had been bandied about. Going forward, we decided that we would be happy to talk with anyone about improvements that they wanted to do, but largely those were going to be decisions voluntarily chosen by the buyer, not choices required for the livability or sale ability of the property.

Making New Friends

There was other work to do. I needed to enlist agent allies in the effort to control the psychology of the sale. Every agent who called me got a return call of thanks for taking an interest in the sale. I also invited each to a special private preview of the property two hours before the first broker open house. I told each agent that I expected a large turn out for the open house and wanted to meet beforehand so that I could personally thank each for taking an interest in the sale and give a private tour.

Anyone inquiring about the repairs (or expressing an opinion about the extent of them) was told that they had come in at around $125,000, based on written estimates provided by half a dozen contractors, and I would be happy to review them with the agent or with their buyers.

Agent Ennui

Almost everyone gave me the same response. They had already seen the property many times. There had been many broker open houses over the years, and there was really no reason to see it again. It was a lovely property but the seller was not serious. Thank you, but it was a waste of their time—and mine, too, in case I wanted to know.

My response was to thank them again for their candor and proceed to reflective listening.

"I know how you feel. I felt the same way when I first learned of the property. But having met with the seller, I know there is going to be a sale here. We sell 93 percent of the properties we list and this property is going to be sold, too.

"Since it is going to be sold, I would like you to be the selling agent who gets the full 3 percent commission.

"Will you indulge me for one more trip to the property, not so much to see it, but to meet me? I'd like very much to meet you so that when you have a buyer, I'll know you and you'll know me. That way we can make this deal happen. What do you say? Would you join me at noon at the property?"

Most agents agreed. I think they were a little intrigued with my approach and wanted to know who this guy was. But to the few who resisted, I said:

"I know how you feel. I feel the same way. But imagine how your reputation will soar, and picture how much business you will get if you can sell a property that no one else has been able to sell in eight years. What would your life be like? Come and meet me so that we can get this job done together. What do you say?"

They came.

So did more than one hundred other agents, many of whom I think came because they had heard from the several dozen with whom I had spoken personally that they should check out "this guy who thinks he can sell *Le Domaine Résistance*." I was glad to have them.

We had prepared a little booklet about the needed repairs. We wanted this issue defused by straight talk so that we could center the discussions on what *had* to be done as opposed to what someone *might* want to do.

On the first page of the booklet we noted the sum total for the repairs and then listed them. In the back were the written estimates. It was a complete package that every agent could give to any buyer who thought the property needed too much work. We had made it easy for the agents to overcome this objection.

Getting the Market Over Its Weariness

We executed a diversion. The focus became not the work needed on the property, but the nutty guys who actually believed they could get a sale done here. Now, the property itself held less curiosity for the agents than the firm with the strange name, LandVest, and the guy with the last name ending in a vowel, me. But we didn't care why they came; we just wanted them to come.

> I had to defuse the issue of the work to be done and impart confidence that a sale would happen.

Their coming was the first victory. We could never control the psychology of the sale without meeting them. I had to look them in the eye and defuse the issue of the work to be done and impart confidence that a sale would happen.

The day of the open house I stood at the door, having memorized the names of each of the two dozen or so agents who had been invited for the personal preview. When they introduced themselves, I greeted them like long lost cousins.

> *"Thank you for being here. I was so glad to get your call. Now picture yourself selling this property. It is going to sell, and I want you to produce the buyer. Imagine the commission and how your reputation is going to soar, how many more sales will result. Now, I know you've been here many times, but just to refresh your memory, I've arranged for you to be taken through again quickly. When you are done, please don't leave without seeing me. I will be right here. I need your opinion and I value it. Will you help to get this sale done?"*

One of our open house attendants then gave them the booklet of repairs and whisked them around for a tour. We graciously ignored the fact that in reality most had never seen the property; we weren't going there. We just wanted to engage them. Every time an objection was made it was followed by, "We know how you feel. We felt the same way when we first saw the property. But it is going to sell and you should be the agent to get the commission."

Co-Opting Feedback

After the tour I guarded the door like a Buckingham Palace guard. It was most important that they not leave without talking to me. I wanted them to honestly tell me what they thought.

What I got was what we expected.

them: "It's a lovely property, but they are not serious sellers."

me: "I know how you feel. I felt the same way, but I assure you they are serious sellers and you should bring us an offer so we can demonstrate that seriousness. Do you have someone to whom you can show it?"

The answer for about ten of the agents was, yes, they did have someone to whom they could present it. Bingo!

Filling the Room

The first problem with this property's psychology, the idea that it needed too much work, was solved. The second problem was now on its way to being solved. The agents, who prior to this open house did not think there was the willingness to make a sale, now were at least open to bringing their buyers in to see the property, some even for a second or third time.

We were beginning to fill the room.

We had traffic.

After the open house Helen Woodbridge came up to me and announced that she had eleven showings. I suggested she announce this fact triumphantly to her office. Why? Because unsurprisingly, none of the showings were from her company.

Indeed, the gloom and skepticism about the property had been so thick at the firm that few agents from her office even came to the open house. Some of this was due to no longer having curiosity about us, having met us at the sales meeting. But largely it was just due to buying in to the argument of "too much work" and the discouragement that comes from believing there is no hope for a sale. We needed her to tell them of the large number of showings to provide them that hope.

By filling the room we now were able to start controlling the psychology of the sale and it started with our own affiliate office.

> By filling the room we now were able to start controlling the psychology of the sale.

Controlling Psychology at the Qualifying

I told Helen that I would personally qualify each buyer and then call her to arrange for the showing. She was delighted that I took this off her plate. For me, I was happy to talk to each and every agent directly. It allowed me yet another attempt to adjust their attitude and another chance to turn them more positive.

Now we had to focus on another issue: buyers' fear to bid because no one else had.

Enter Stepladder Marketing

The buyers for *Le Domaine Résistance* were much like buyers who come to the auction and find they are the only one in the room. The whole listing shouted "sole buyer syndrome." Leery buyers asked, Why hadn't it sold in eight years? What was wrong with it? Once we overcame the broker skepticism we had to work on their buyers to raise their comfort level to act.

And how do we get sophisticated buyers to feel more comfortable to bid? You know the answer: other buyers.

Almost every buyer whose agent had requested a showing was qualified, and when I spoke with the agent, I was clear on what we wanted here: cash offers. The property was magnificent and well priced; therefore, I didn't want to bother with time-consuming financing contingencies. I was looking for a cash buyer and a quick closing.

> And how do we get sophisticated buyers to feel more comfortable to bid? You know the answer: other buyers.

For me, the idea of cash offers and quick closing was meant to counter two impressions. First, I wanted to boldly tell the buyers through the agents that there was no reason for anything else. Pricing was right, repairs had been quantified, the property was prime and magnificent, and the property would sell. It was a good deal.

The second reason for cash and quick closing was due to the suspicion that, if we did not produce a full-price offer with no financing contingency and a thirty-to-sixty-day closing, we might not ever have a deal. I wasn't going to say that publicly but in my gut I sensed the possibility of my seller having a change of heart. Because of that I did not want to get the psychology off to the wrong start by having agents encourage their buyers to put in offers with contingencies that in the end were not going to create a sale and earn a commission. Anything less than a cash sale with a quick close was just going to waste time.

A Little Chutzpah Can Do Wonders

Within the brokerage community my chutzpah created a certain shock that was extremely helpful, especially since first impressions are often lasting. The agents soon started buzzing, "This property has been stagnating for eight years, and this guy wants only cash offers with no financing contingency? Boy, that guy is not only confident, but a little cocky!" Yes, I wanted to get the property sold, get paid, and get a reputation for being serious. Therefore, why not ask for the order right up front? So, I did.

Keeping the Audience Alert and Informed

To control the positive psychology of the brokerage community and overcome their skepticism, I kept the agents constantly informed.

The staff used fax machines and snail mail like a blitzkrieg (e-mail blasts did not exist yet). Initially we sent out a mailing to more than five hundred agents (even to those who didn't show up at the open house) just to thank them for their interest. Then we sent another letter telling them that we had eleven showings scheduled for the property and urged them to bring their buyers.

What Were We Doing?

We were filling the room *and* ensuring that everyone knew it was happening, since unlike the auction room, our virtual room did not allow buyers and agents to see each other. After eight years of unsuccessful marketing, i.e., of the room being empty (which everyone knew), we now wanted everyone to know and feel the buzz around *Le Domaine Résistance*, a buzz that came from being in a room filling up with buyers.

Initially, this constant and continuous communication was shocking to the brokerage community, which had never seen anything quite like it. We were trumpeting a stale listing and everyone's involvement in it as if it were the most exciting listing to have ever come to market.

The initial bewilderment morphed into a kind of weekly fascination with what was going on with the property. Our barrage of letters, postcards, and telephone calls created a transparency that was surprising and then oddly welcome. We new guys were startlingly public in how we sold real estate, which caused everyone to talk about us and, of course, the property.

The Orchestration

After every showing I personally called the agents and asked what their buyer thought. Most were positive. Some felt the property was too much for them, the upkeep being more than they anticipated. But overall, the impressions were positive and led to a conversation I'd have over and over:

ME: *"So, will they be making us an offer?"*
AGENT: *"Where do you think this is going to sell?"*
ME: *"It will sell for the asking price—it's a fabulous property and worth it. The asking price represents clear defensible value. Do you remember those gorgeous gates? That winding drive? The house, perfectly nestled behind the hill? Do you remember the slight gasp you felt when you entered the courtyard?"*
AGENT: *"But no one is going to bid the asking price! It has been on for eight years."*

I then always asked for the offer.

ME: *"Then what is your buyer willing to pay? Give me that offer and I will present it and we will get a deal done."*

This dialogue is a bit of a script ending with a singular encouragement: *give me an offer.* In the case of this property, it was imperative and I was desperate for an offer. Why?

Comfort Through Other Bids

Just like the auctioneer needing an opening bid, I needed to establish that, after eight years, someone wanted this property. The focus turned from raising the comfort level and controlling the psychology of the *agents* to doing the same for the *buyers*. I needed an offer within the first four to six weeks of the marketing campaign. If no one raised a hand to bid, I was in trouble.

Just like the auctioneer needing an opening bid, I needed to establish that, after eight years, someone wanted this property.

Consequently, I was on the phone non-stop, soliciting an offer from any agent who had brought a buyer. After all, there had been eleven showings and the brokerage community was positive about the property. Daily I urged agents to have their buyers throw in a bid.

Given how long this property had been on the market, we had a little more time to get the first offer than the usual first two to three weeks. But with this listing, it was even more critical that we produce an offer. Failure to demonstrate that someone wanted the property would confirm all the fears and beliefs of the brokerage community, and showings would trail off. Without an offer we would be back to the property no one had wanted in eight years.

But if we got an offer, it would be more than a dose of positive energy. It would be viewed as something close to a miracle, and my audience of weekly viewers would likely tune in more and maybe even cheer the whole process on.

The answer is "stepladder marketing." Consider it a powerful part of your *power marketing* arsenal. We needed to get to the top of the ladder, the asking price, by starting on the lowest rung, much like the auctioneer starts low to get high. Although we wanted the property to sell for the highest price, we first had to establish a base price. And, more fundamentally, we had to establish that someone wanted to own the property.

The Starting Bid

I got what I wanted, an offer of $550,000, cash, no contingencies, closing in sixty days. Well, I thought to myself, at least they got the terms right.

With this offer, however, we were off. I duly presented the offer to the seller, who duly rejected it. We went back to the buyer, who asked for a counter-offer. The seller countered with the asking price (surprise!) and the buyer balked. We called the agent for the buyer and asked if he would come up in price. He would not. We persisted, but the buyer was done.

Overcoming Sole Buyer Syndrome

The moment our negotiation ended (it only took a day), we sent out a media blitz. The message was simple: an offer had been made for the property. It was too low to successfully take the property, but if you have a buyer interested, please bring her forward at this time.

My phone rang off the hook as every agent called to ask how much the offer was for. I said that since it was still possible that the buyer would come up in price, I couldn't disclose the price, but I asked, enthusiastically, whether the agent wanted to present an offer.

The news of our offer and undisclosed price spread like wildfire in the brokerage community and helped to create dozens more showings. Everyone was speculating on how much the offer was for, and Helen was instructed not to say. I wanted the guessing to continue because it kept the buzz alive and focused agent attention on our listing.

I began to receive calls from other agents indicating that their buyers wanted to bid and asking for instructions as to where to come in. Always my response was the same: only the asking price was sure to take the property.

We received a second offer in the seventh week. It was for $500,000. Our response to that offer was delight. Why?

- It made the first offer look good and that was hard to do.
- It was a second bidder, precisely the goal.

When I called the agent back, I informed her that we would be presenting the offer immediately, which we did. Our seller quickly laughed and turned down the offer. I asked,

"What would you like me to tell the buyer?"

She indicated that we should say that we already had a higher offer.

That was exactly the response I wanted to deliver, and did. As you can imagine, this started a dialogue between agents with me as to the price point we were talking about. When the other agent wanted to know how much higher the bid was, I told her that I would call her back. First, I wanted to call the initial agent whose buyer had made the $550,000 offer to tell him we had new interest and inquire whether that buyer wanted to re-enter the bidding. The first offerer declined to make a second offer. She was not interested except at the $550,000 level. I repeated that such an offer had been turned down. *"They aren't going higher,"* I was told. *"May I take that to mean our negotiations are over?"* I asked. *"Yes,"* she said.

Up the Ladder We Go

Asking that last question is essential because I do not want to "shop" any offer, nor ever get the reputation for doing so. As long as the negotiations are still open I do not feel the price offered should be disclosed. But once negotiations end, I feel it is perfectly fine to disclose what had been turned down by the seller. In this case I went back to the second buyer and said that we had already turned down $550,000.

The agent's response was not surprising. She asked if $600,000 would take it. I demurred but told her to make the offer to find out. Her buyer did and the offer was turned down, as expected. But now we had TWO offers on the property in two months, and that was two more than anyone had ever known about in eight years. At this point you can imagine what I did. I called everyone with the news that there had now been two offers on the property.

While the speculation continued as to the price point where the offers had been made, I continued to decline to comment on them.

This process continued for fourteen offers on the property. I will not go through them all, but some increased their increments by $50,000 and some by $25,000 and some by $10,000. Throughout the laborious process we continued to make sure we did not violate anyone's confidentiality, but we also made sure that if the negotiations were ended and

> I called everyone with the news that there had now been two offers on the property.

the buyer would not go higher, the other offerers knew what had been turned down.

Regarding price, I repeated *ad nauseum* that the only thing that we could be sure would take the property was full price, all cash, with a thirty-to-sixty-day closing. In the end, we had three bidders who stayed in the game. Everyone was told the same: the first to come to full asking price would take the property.

Along the way, the number of offers was always disclosed. We certainly wanted everyone to know that there was interest, lots of it. A market watching a property that had no offers in eight years needed to see that. We even wanted to give every impression of a bidding frenzy.

All along the way, at each price point, the buyers' comfort levels were constantly raised by the presence of other bidders. What we had established was that not only did someone want this property, but four people wanted it, then eight, then twelve, and so forth. We had successfully controlled the psychology of the sale to raise the comfort level of the agents and their buyers to the point where we had multiple interest in the property. We were pulling everyone up the rungs of the ladder, hoping to get someone to the top.

The eight-year marketing curse of *Le Domaine Résistance* now had been broken.

Hitting the Goal

In the end we had three buyers bidding simultaneously and we got to our desired goal: an offer for $995,000, all cash, closing in thirty days. This rookie luxury marketer had done what the agents said was impossible. I was proud. We were now due a commission. It was time to call my client with the wonderful news.

What I then learned was that my client did not want to take anything less than $1.1 million, with the desire to net $1 million for herself.

I thought someone had taken a spike and put it into my heart.

I had just done the impossible. I had perfectly orchestrated fourteen bidders to accomplish what no one else had in eight years. I had wowed the brokerage community, who had already brought us in on a half dozen other listings to market, and I had visions of sales dancing in my head—until I talked with my seller. While I was despondent, my mentor, Wade Staniar was not.

"Let's talk to her attorney," he advised. "She does not have to sell. She just has to pay us our commission."

The Importance of the Listing Agreement

It was at that moment that I learned the wisdom of a good listing agreement, and it is why I have included a chapter on the essentials of such in this book. Wade's wisdom in making sure the agreement required us to be paid if we had done our job, now saved the day. All the work we had done, all the marketing chutzpah, and all the great efforts could have been down the drain, had we not been secured by a rock-solid listing agreement that was focused on making sure we got paid.

We did talk to our client's attorney. We also talked directly to our client. We told her that we knew how she must feel. We would feel the same way, but we had been hired to do a job and we had just accomplished it. While it was not necessary to accept the offer and sell the property, it was necessary to pay us. Our commission of $99,500 was due and payable.

In the end, the terms of the deal were renegotiated, extending the closing date, but only after we had received agreement from the seller's attorney that our listing contract would be honored and we would be paid.

Le Domaine Résistance was a marketing triumph with the core lessons of *power marketing* learned. Its sale served to establish our reputation on the North Shore. Within three years we were doing almost half of the top sales in that market.

The Takeaway _____

- By quantifying in advance the work that was to be done, objections were contained and comfort raised.

- Interest was revitalized and piqued by inviting, reaching out, and cajoling everyone in the brokerage community to participate in the sale, and insisting a sale would occur.

- By encouraging any offer, we obtained a low bid that helped change the psychology and establish that someone wanted to own this property. We then built upon that fact to generate additional offers.

- The presence of multiple offers was key to raising the comfort level of each additional buyer (and the agents) to bid higher.

- "Filling the room" with buyers allowed us to orchestrate the bidding to one all-important point in time: having multiple buyers bidding simultaneously.

- Constant communication with the brokerage community publicly notified them of additional people in the room at every step.

- We demonstrated that smart buyers will indeed pay, but only when they know others are bidding, too.

- A well-worded listing agreement can save the day (and our commission).

8

Listings that Explain It All: Clarendon Court

The second *power marketing* story comes from my listing and sale of Clarendon Court, the magnificent and notorious home on Bellevue Avenue in Newport, Rhode Island that belonged to Martha ("Sunny") and Claus von Bülow.

This twenty-room mansion was featured in the opening aerial shots of the 1956 Hollywood movie, High Society, starring Bing Crosby, Frank Sinatra, and Grace Kelly and was built in 1904 by the noted architect Horace Trumbauer, who also created the fabled "Elms" mansion and the neighboring estate, "Miramar." It is an exact copy in design and measurements of Hedley House, County Durham, England, built in 1710 by Colin Campbell, the architect of Buckingham Palace.

In December 1980 this Newport "cottage" was the scene of an alleged murder attempt on Mrs. von Bülow. The two children from her first marriage to Prince Alfie von Auersperg, the Princess Annie-Laurie von Auersperg and Prince Alexander von Auersperg, suspected their stepfather, Claus von Bülow, of trying to kill their mother with an overdose of insulin. An insulin-encrusted hypodermic needle was discovered hidden in a black bag in Mr. von Bülow's bedroom closet.

His 1982 trial, covered daily by the world press, resulted in his conviction and a sentence of thirty years in jail. However, in 1985, Mr. von Bülow's legal team, led by Harvard law professor Alan M. Dershowitz, appealed successfully based on the fact that a search warrant had not been issued when state officials tested the contents of the black bag. They argued that the only possible way for the hypodermic needle to have become encrusted with insulin was if it had been deliberately dipped. This seemed to suggest that von Bülow might have been framed. Given that reasonable doubt had now been inserted into the case, on June 10, 1985, the jury acquitted him of all charges.

> If, prior to Clarendon Court, we considered our *power marketing* "Coke bottle marketing," Clarendon Court caused us to rename it "Champagne marketing."

Of all the properties that I have handled, Clarendon Court had, by far, the highest profile. It remains one of the most famous properties in the world because of so many celebrated aspects. Indeed, novelist and *Vanity Fair* reporter Dominick Dunne called Mrs. von Bülow's saga "one of the most sensational stories in the annals of American and international high society."[21] There would later be a movie version of the events, *Reversal of Fortune,* with Jeremy Irons as von Bülow and Glenn Close as his wife, Sunny. Dunne's television episode on the event would replay for years in his TV series, *Power, Privilege and Justice.*

I listed the property on behalf of the family early in the spring of 1988. One would have thought that, given its fame, Clarendon Court would have had an enormous market of would-be buyers. But the property's upkeep ran to almost a million dollars a year. The fact that an attempted murder was alleged to have been committed in the master bedroom created a worrisome psychological impediment. The concern was that the combination could send the property in the way of so many Newport estates: to be donated.

The Lead

I am often asked how I got a lead on such a property.

My focus in the 1980s was the network of real estate trust officers at major New York bank trust departments. Those clients consisted of about fifteen bank trust officers largely centered in Manhattan who controlled, through their departments, hundreds of millions of dollars of real estate assets, which were often upscale homes. As a service, we offered to act as adviser-consultants for the valuation, market research, management, marketing, and sometimes the disposition of such assets. Once a calendar quarter, my colleagues and I would call upon the trust officers.

LESSON: SOMETIMES NO JOB IS TOO SMALL

I always mentioned to the trust and estate officers who were my clients that there was no property too small or too difficult to speak with me about—and we often did. One such client's needs ranged from determining the value of fourteen gas stations in the Southwest to valuing some tiny properties in St. Lucie, Florida that, altogether, did not amount to more than $100,000. For me the size did not matter: I always made sure that I was someone who could be contacted to discuss anything.

You might say what goes around comes around.

In addition to the minor consultations above, this trust officer also brought me in on the sale of John Wayne's former home in Newport Beach, California, where I helped to find a suitable agent. I was also brought in to consult on the estate of another client who had left not only $400M in trust, but real estate all over the globe that now had to be valued and ultimately sold.

I was even brought in on a property in Switzerland owned by a relative of Napoleon Bonaparte that had been deed restricted and could be sold only to another head of state.

Finally, and notably for my career, I was called with a property emanating from the estate of Seward Johnson of Johnson & Johnson fame. When Mr. Johnson died, two of his Italian villas were left to his wife who decided to sell the homes.

Additionally, we also called upon the trust and estate attorneys of major law firms handling the assets of America's wealthy—a tactic with known results: Dick Perkins, our president, had a close working relationship with one attorney for many notable people, including Jacqueline Kennedy Onassis. That one contact allowed Dick to handle assembling multitudinous parcels of land that ultimately formed Mrs. Onassis' Martha's Vineyard estate.

Through bank trust officers Wade Staniar handled the sale of highly sensitive large parcels for descendants of the William Rockefeller family at their Bay Pond retreat in the Adirondacks. He also oversaw prestigious lot sales in Osterville, Massachusetts, on behalf of the Arthur Vining Davis family. In Greenwich, John Coburn handled the sale of the Gimbel (the department store) family estate, among other notable properties.

A Little Relationship Goes a Long Way

The Johnson property had complex ownership that spanned two conti-
nents and several entities and was extremely difficult to value because
of the inaccuracy of recorded selling prices in the Italian public records.

I had to admit to my trust officer client that I knew little about valuing and marketing real estate in Italy, but I appreciated the problem and
I promised to provide the names of some people who might help. After
doing research and finding very few names, I submitted three contacts.
I forewarned that they did not come with my recommendation. Indeed,
I admitted I knew nothing about them except that my research indicated a claim to know something about international real estate.

About a week later my trust officer client called and asked me to
come to the office. When I arrived I was asked if I could advise on the
sale. As it turns out the three people I referred had each boasted of
having international marketing expertise. The stories, however, did not
impress. Instead, the client was more reassured by prior experiences
with me, which, when combined with the willingness always to help,
overcame the candor of lacking Italian experience.

I was hired to write a market report on how to sell property in Italy,
the legal implications of a transfer, the financing issues involved, recommendations on property management, and maximizing value. But most
importantly I wrote a section valuing the property and suggesting how
to market it to get the highest price.

After reading the report, the client called and asked me to handle
the sale. Again, I was reluctant. I had never handled a sale in Italy and
did not know even if legally I could. But I was reminded of our policy at
LandVest: unlike many consultants who leave implementation to others, it was our policy always to carry out the recommendations we had
been hired to provide. I said I would talk to my senior management.
They, in turn, were genuinely concerned about our ability to deliver
results for a property so far away but reluctantly agreed, acknowledging
it as a necessity of our policy.

With that agreement, I was off marketing my first luxury property
abroad and one of the most expensive properties ever offered in Italy.
A year later, I completed the sale and a twenty-five year international
marketing career was launched. It led to such assignments as consulting on the Schlumberger family's palace in Sintra, Portugal, consulting
for the U.S. State Department after the fall of the Berlin Wall as one of
their first foreign real estate advisors in Eastern Europe, and helping

to start the Eastern European Real Property Foundations (now the International Real Property Foundation) on whose Board of Directors I still sit. Out of these and many other international marketing experiences now emerges yet another book: *Global Connections: Marketing Homes Internationally.*

Clarendon Court

The lead for Clarendon Court came exactly the same way as these other leads, but this time from Chemical Bank, where Mrs. von Bülow's trusts were located. Her trust officer was Morris Gurley, who was also in charge of her estate. Don Fox and Sheridan Nofer, with whom I had developed a good relationship, worked the real estate trust department at the bank. The property was technically owned by the "Committee for the non-trust property," which was made up of Chemical Bank and Sims Farr, a senior partner at the esteemed New York law firm of White and Case.

One day Don Fox called and said he had a property to sell and that he wanted me to come and do a listing presentation for it, with one caveat: it was highly unlikely that I would get the listing or handle the sale. The family, he said, were inclined toward a packaged approach of having one firm handle the contents and the house together, and the beneficiaries were inclined toward another firm. However, under New York State trust law, the bank had to interview at least two competent and credible brokers for possible hiring.

Don reassured me that in return for my time I would be uppermost in his thoughts for other opportunities. I agreed. He then told me that the listing presentation would be to the bank, the beneficiaries, and their lawyers.

My jaw dropped when he told me the property was Clarendon Court. This was the most infamous and talked about property in America, and possibly the world.

Pricing Clarendon Court

To prepare for the presentation we had to try to figure out what the property might be worth. My colleague Chris Burr worked with me on the pricing. We were allowed into the property for a preview conducted by the star of the von Bülow trial, Maria Schallhammer, the Austrian maid who had demonstrated her loyalty to Mrs. von Bülow.

After reviewing the plot plan, walking the boundaries, cataloging the rooms and outbuildings as well as the amenities, we went through the exact process described in Chapter 4. We began with the underlying land value. We made a list of sales where a property sold and was torn down, presuming that the buyer bought it for its land value. We looked at parcels of land currently available. With all of this distilled, we came up with an underlying value range for the land.

We then calculated the replacement value of the house, the improvements, outbuildings, and amenities. We adjusted for age and condition. We then compared this range of prices to about five years of property sales in Newport over $1M. Not surprisingly, it was not a long list. Research indicated there had never been a sale over $1.8M, and no previous sale was of property in any way comparable to the magnificence of Clarendon Court. We then looked at and compared the property to others currently available.

Through Chris's sleuth work we also came upon a valuable piece of information. A contact at a local brokerage office said that the competing firm that was likely to get the listing was recommending a listing price to the bank of no more than $2.1M.

That price would be a record price for Newport and one, our source indicated, not likely to be attained. The source also confirmed that the associated parties were worried that there might even be no buyer for the property and that it, like so many other grand Newport mansions, would have to be donated to the historic preservation trust or some other such organization. And given that it was soon after the stock market crash of 1987, the local and national climate was in no mood for record pricing of anything.

Gauging Motivation

Gauging motivation is one of the seven steps of pricing. Did we even have a motivated seller? At first glance the motivation of the seller was discouraging. Claus von Bülow really did not want the property sold at all. He and Sunny had meticulously furnished it, and he preferred that it be retained. Their daughter, Cosima, seemed to feel the same but was ready to go along with whatever was decided. The two von Auersperg children wanted it sold, not appreciating the glare of the headlines any longer. But certainly there was no financial necessity; even the $1 million a year to maintain the estate was not a problem.

Given the challenges—no urgency to sell, the small/nonexistent and illiquid market—we asked these questions:

- Would the sellers therefore allow the property to be sold for what might be a small number?
- Would they just hold out for obtaining a price acceptable to them?
- Could this be a property that might stay on the market for years?
- If it did not produce bidders at the right price, might they even withdraw it from the market?
- Would the divisions within the family about a sale lead to a stalemate?
- Who had the upper hand, the children or Mr. von Bülow, and how could we determine that?
- Were we asking people to buy a white elephant, which, when it came time to sell, would leave them wanting?

Surely, if any property needed *power marketing*, this was it. The market was tiny and tepid, concern was high, and doubts matched those concerns. But our desire to list one of the most celebrated, beautiful—albeit ill-famed—properties in the world was strong, and we were determined.

Our Considerations

Since this would be one of the most intensely reported and closely watched sales in America, it also ran the risk of being the most reported and watched failure in America. We asked whether such a high profile failure would put the bank in the spotlight and whether it wanted its trust department to be tainted with such a failure. Given what the family had been through, we also wondered if they could deal with the additional stigma of nobody wanting their property. A failure would make tabloid headlines of the first order and cause more family drama.

Therefore, we conjectured that the family was committed to getting out of the limelight and out of the press and to putting the spotlight onto someone else. In effect, we were wagering that the property's very fame and notoriety would not allow for a public failure and a sale at some price was inevitable. In effect, we had a motivated seller.

What Was that Price?

In evaluating the core or book value, we noted that the land consisted of about seven acres with 680 feet fronting Bellevue Avenue, lined with high stone walls covered in espaliered yew that ensured privacy. There was also 750 feet of direct water frontage on Narragansett Bay. There was the matter of the tourist walkway "Cliff Walk" between the ocean and estate backyards—but fortunately, it had been built below the property to prevent trespassing, preserving the privacy of the owners. That added value.

The von Bülows also had purchased an adjacent property "Gull Rock" once a rambling Queen Anne–style cottage, which they demolished to provide not only a sweeping vista of the ocean but a broad golf hole that could double as a croquet course. The Gull Rock parcel was a separate lot that could be sold off without interfering with the integrity of the main house, providing additional flexibility, and thereby additional investment value.

So what was the land worth? There had been some waterfront land sales (sans houses) along the coast that had approached $1M. Therefore we assumed the land was worth a minimum of $1M and a high range of probably 40 to 60 percent more, or $1.4M to $1.6M. Given the location and a possible subdividable lot, we settled on $1.5M—low by today's standards, but considerable back then.

The house was a three-story English Georgian home done in Palladian style and built of stone masonry with steel I-beam construction and a copper roof. At the back of the house was a colonnaded open veranda facing a pool and ocean. The house— almost 12,000 square feet of living space—featured hardwood herringbone floors and ornamented triple crown moldings with dentils and friezes.

> We had defensible value, something we could argue credibly to sophisticated and informed buyers...This still left open the price we should ask for such value.

The entrance had a grand marble stairway with elaborate wrought-iron balusters capped in mahogany. The second floor had two bedrooms in each of two wings, and the third floor had five smaller bedrooms. On the first floor was the famous master bedroom, where the alleged murder attempt occurred. A perfectly proportioned living room extended from the front courtyard of the house to the back ocean views. The dining room comfortably sat twenty to forty for dinner. The proportions and scale throughout the house had a twentieth century sensibility that homes like "Marble House," several doors to the north, and Vanderbilt's "The Breakers" did not.

It was unimaginable to us that one could replicate the house for less than $250 to $300 a square foot. Nonetheless, we put a more conservative replacement value below this range of $200 per square foot, or $2.4M for just the 12,000-square-foot house. Still, our valuation of the house without the land was more than had ever been paid for a property with land in Newport.

Other improvements and amenities included:

- A two-story Queen Anne-styled brick carriage house built of steel I-beam construction with a slate roof. It had five apartments (most with water views) ranging in size from efficiency to duplex and garage bays for four to six vehicles.

- A brick-walled cutting garden in eighteenth-century English style, containing several thousand bulbs of heritage flowers.

- Extensive mature landscaping featured Japanese black pines, rhododendron, autumn olive, beech trees, and numerous other exquisite plantings that were bordered by privet hedges and Japanese roses.

- A 44-by-105-foot heated pool with working fountains that framed the stunning views to the sea.

The rental income from the carriage house apartments was enough to at least defray the $33,000 of taxes on the property. We valued the carriage house and its five apartments at a low of $300,000 to a maximum of $500,000, settling on $400,000 for an average. We valued the perimeter walls, the plantings, the pool and fountains, and the mature landscaping at a conservative $250,000 to $400,000.

In the end we took all these ranges and arrived at a total core value of $4,550,000 to replace what was there, not including the "convenience value"—the premium for its being in move-in condition (as discussed earlier, this has a special value in resort markets like Newport). We put a (conservative) 10 percent premium for its convenience value, believing it would take at least two years to replicate such a house. This added $450,000 a year ($900,000 of value over two years). It was a stretch, but it was an accurate stretch.

This brought the total value represented by Clarendon Court up to $5,005,000 to $5,450,000 before factoring in the celebrity value, which we guesstimated at $500,000. When all was calculated, we felt we could articulate and defend a core value of $5.5 million to $6 million.

This did not mean we felt that we could get that number. In fact, we felt that such a number would scare the brokerage community and likely hurt the possibility of a sale. What we felt we had here was defensible value, something that we could argue credibly to sophisticated and informed buyers and that they and their advisers would understand. This still left open the question of the price we should ask for such value.

Determining the Asking Price

Our value analysis then took an unlikely turn. We focused on guessing how much of a *discount* from the defensible core value of $5.5 to $6 million a smart buyer would pay. Discount? Clarendon Court? Linking this property to the idea of a discount seemed startlingly incompatible.

But we knew what you now know, that nothing raises the comfort level of a rich buyer more than a bargain. By looking at Clarendon Court like a balance sheet of a company, weighing its assets and liabilities to get at its core book value, we were simulating buying a company for a discount to its "book value."

To create the discount and finalize an asking price for the property, we slashed a third off our core book value, believing it might bring us to a tempting price. At a minimum it was a credible and defensible one. This brought us to a range of $3,630,000 to $3,960,000.

> By looking at Clarendon Court like a balance sheet of a company, weighing its assets and liabilities to get at its core book value, we were simulating buying a company for a discount to its "book value."

Would we get it? We certainly hoped we could find a buyer who was insightful enough to recognize the core value, be delighted by the discount, and maybe, with the right competition, even pay more.

On the downside, if we could only get 50 percent of the core value, or just $2.5M to $3M, the sale would still set a record price in Newport, even with the discount.

In the end we settled on an asking price of $3.95M and were ready to go to the family and the bank. We, of course, knew that the ultimate price would not be based on anyone's valuation but rather on the broker's marketing strategy. Hopefully, it would be ours.

Lesson: to appeal to the rich, a property must be presented in the form of a discount to core value, even when asking a record price.

When you take a discussion from the price a buyer is willing to pay to how large a discount from book value that buyer is willing to bid, you have taken the discussion to a place the rich like to be.

By not just looking at the past sales within Newport (what everyone else was doing and thinking), but by calculating the component, convenience, and celebrity value, we had come up with the sales rationale we needed for smart buyers.

While others were fretting over whether Clarendon Court could get a new high price in Newport, we focused on how much of a discount from intrinsic core value we might get. Given the climate after the stock market crash of 1987, this was exactly the rationale we needed for buyers. A discount, we reasoned, is how we would create an urgency to act among the few buyers we expected, all of whom did not have to buy. The realization now gripped us that to get a record price we had to talk in terms of a record bargain.

The Listing Appointment

The meeting room at Chemical Bank was in a classic—and intimidating—mahogany boardroom. At these meetings I usually do not like to take my seat until I know where everyone else is sitting. But I was asked to sit at the head, with Chris Burr and Bob Borden on either side of me facing each other. Don Fox welcomed us cordially, while several attorneys, including the family's attorney, arrived. Everyone chatted a bit except for me, nervously harboring my private terror as I contemplated my first presentation to celebrity clients. I sensed that everyone had an inkling that they were wasting our time.

After another fifteen minutes, all were present. The von Auersperg children shared a place at the far end of the table, at the head opposite me. There were several chairs gapping between them and the rest of us. The space between them and me was about 20 feet. I was now to begin the listing presentation of a lifetime with some of the worst body language one could imagine.

Sims Farr, the children's attorney from the prestigious law firm of White and Case, reminded everyone that we were here to get a second opinion on the pricing and marketing of Clarendon Court. He also reminded everyone of the highly confidential nature of the meeting, noting that nothing had been decided. Farr then turned to look down the table at me and asked me to begin.

Borden, realizing my jitters and knowing that I would probably start by talking too much rather than by asking questions, leaned over the table and said,

"Before David begins, perhaps, Sims, you and the bank and Ala and Alex can tell us any thoughts you have about the process."

It was a classic "Whoopen" question ("Wide Open"). As the senior member of the team, he knew well that if anyone could get away with asking it, he could.

Farr immediately spoke of his concern about the high maintenance cost of the property. Farr's colleague, Winthrop ("Win") Rutherfurd concurred but wanted the high maintenance put into perspective, indicating that one of the reasons for such a high expense was that the property was so meticulously maintained. He hoped this lack of deferred maintenance would be viewed as a positive for any buyer.

Borden and Burr asked other questions, which I knew were all designed to keep everyone else talking first. After about fifteen minutes, Farr, becoming impatient with the details and small talk, blurted out,

"What are we going to get for this property?"

All eyes, including Borden's, turned to me, who had been silent throughout. Borden signaled that it was now time to say what we came to say.

"The price you will get is a function of the marketing you choose today." I then paused to let my words sit heavily on the table. We all waited for a reaction. There was no need for a second sentence until someone talked.

Don Fox broke the silence, asking what I meant.

"Clarendon Court is one of the premier properties in America. It has all the potential to set a record price for Newport, but only if the marketing that is chosen today is commensurate with the quality of the property. There is no question about the property, its value, or its renown. The only question is whether the marketing can raise the comfort level of the buyers to a point that they will pay a price appropriate to its immense value and stature."

More silence, broken by someone's question of how we could do that.

Our competition was a national and international firm; it was important for me to dilute the most compelling reason to hire them: their global reach.

"We will market to the whole world through a coordinated campaign that involves the media, all other brokers and agents, a targeted advertising and mailing campaign, and orchestrated showings.

"Once those buyers are found—and for this property they will be found—everything will turn on whether the marketers know what to do with those buyers. Our focus has to be not on the easy part—the worldwide reach—but the aspect that involves real expertise: orchestrating the comfort level of multiple buyers to bid for this property all at the same time."

Borden now spoke and explained that the market for Clarendon Court was extremely small. That fact would make the buyers nervous about resale someday and about whether, upon a resale, they would be able to recover what they paid. It was our job to help them to overcome their nervousness by presenting a defensible value, and then to create comfort by demonstrating broad interest and competition.

Filling the Room

We then explained our marketing strategy. In order to demonstrate multiple buyer interest in the property, we would arrange the showings so that no one would have more than one hour for an initial appointment, and most buyers would see other buyers coming before and after them. When the 11 a.m. buyer arrived, she would see the 10 a.m. buyer leave, and at the end of her house tour she would see the 12 p.m. buyer arriving. In this way every buyer would be aware of others and recognize they were not alone. The whole point was to make sure all buyers knew there was competition and the room was filling up.

> Every buyer would be aware of others and recognize they were not alone. The point was to make sure all buyers knew there was competition and the room was filling up.

I explained that in order to get the buyers bidding simultaneously we would set a date some six to eight weeks after marketing began for showings to commence. This meant that no one could view the property until the showings began, nor could anyone buy the property during the six to eight week marketing period. Everyone wants something more when he cannot have it, I explained. In this way we would pique buyer interest and then funnel that interest into a forced narrow decision-making window of time, after which we would set a date for receipt of all written offers. The showing and decision-making process would, in effect, replicate the room of an auction house where bidders would not be allowed to buy until they became aware of one another's presence and felt comforted from knowing that others wanted the property.

Because the market for Clarendon Court was extremely small, our allowing buyers to be aware of each other would also help to overcome the nervousness they felt about the prospect for a resale someday.

More lengthy and intensive second showings would be allowed after the first. We explained again that we needed that first set of tightly scheduled showings to demonstrate to buyers that they were not alone—that we had multiple and extensive interest in the property. We would replicate this strategy on the second showings, too, if there were any. Finally, the certain date for the bids would help to create an urgency for buyers to act.

Borden then explained that we usually dubbed the marketing phase "Coke bottle marketing." In this phase a day is set for the property to come to market, cooperation and compensation are offered to all agents, and mailings, advertising, and public relations commence. It is during this period that we "shake the Coke bottle" to generate a fizz of interest in the property and bring focus to it.

Borden then announced that we had renamed this strategy "Champagne marketing" in honor of Clarendon Court. There would be the same shaking of the marketing bottle during the initial six to eight week period, but in this case it would be a metaphorical Champagne bottle that would pop at the end of the marketing period, hopefully with a flurry of offers and a celebrated sale.

Everyone smiled. We had not planned that phrase; it seemed to come to Borden as we sat at the table. In hindsight, it provided exactly the kind of customization of the marketing process appropriate for such a special property, and its originality pleased everyone, not the least of whom was me.

The Pricing Issue

Up to this point we hadn't talked about pricing. Rather, the whole focus of the presentation had been on marketing. Then Farr again asked us to address the pricing issue.

"We have spent considerable time pricing Clarendon Court, and we recommend an asking price of 3.95 million dollars," I said. "We think it is a credible and defensible asking price. But remember, the selling price will not be set by us but by the market we create."

I then explained how we had thought through the valuation and how we would position Clarendon Court with an intrinsic core value of almost $6M, pointing out that our recommended asking price represented a one-third discount from this core value.

Bidders would not be allowed to buy until they became aware of one another's presence and felt comforted from knowing that others wanted the property

"We think we can raise the comfort level of the buyers by articulating this demonstrable value and focusing them on the discount they are enjoying. We also think we can sell the discount to brokers and the press.

In this way we feel we can control opinions on the record pricing in a positive way."

Around the table, heads began to nod. Eyes glanced at other eyes. Some whispers started along the side. Farr asked Borden whether he concurred in this asking price. He said he did. He looked at Burr, who had spent so much time researching it, and he, too, nodded his agreement.

Farr then stated slightly incredulously that we were talking about getting almost $2M more than what others had told them to expect. It was the first sign that Burr's research about our competition's recommended pricing was correct.

Reminding him that pricing is a function of marketing, I said,

"We think our marketing will get you the highest price. Whether it is 3.95 million dollars or lower or higher will be determined by the market. But we know how to create markets and orchestrate them to get successful results. We strongly feel that 3.95 million dollars is a credible and defensible price and we're ready to go with it."

There was a long pause, followed by some whispered comments around the table while our team sat silently. Then Don Fox stood up and thanked us for coming. We said goodbye to everyone and left the room, not knowing what the verdict would be.

I have no idea what occurred in the boardroom after we left. Later I learned that under New York State fiduciary law it was required to list a property for the highest price a responsible and credible broker believed he could achieve. If so, that may have played a part in the decision.

Whatever. Don Fox called me the next day with the news that we would be listing Clarendon Court. He asked me to send a listing contract.

When Farr called to remind us of the embargo on publicity, he emphasized something we had presumed and counted on, but never had quite confirmed. He reminded me that they wanted Clarendon Court sold, emphasizing that the property could not stay on the market for an extended period of time. He gave me the opportunity to revise the price, saying that this was the last chance to do so.

His fear that it might not sell was what I needed to hear. Now we knew that we had a motivated seller. Our bet that they would take the price the market offered seemed correct.

Marketing Preparations

To begin the marketing, Burr and I spent a day at the house and went through every square foot while taking meticulous notes. The purpose of this visit was to gather visceral details, such as how the light came through the windows, when it shone on the house, and at precisely which hours. I tried to get the feel of the house, the emotional senses it gave off so as to better highlight these features when talking with agents and buyers. Having this information might also allow us to deflect conversation about the alleged murder attempt.

We framed a dozen potential photographs to determine which rooms we would feature in the brochure, without invading the privacy of the family or providing anything salacious for the media.

We hired one of our finest photographers, Michael Mathers, known for his *Architectural Digest* shoots. He did exemplary work with lighting, which was critical because we were shooting in the low light days of late winter, whereas for brochures we normally would have looked to dusk or evening shots with light coming out of the windows. Such shots would also have taken the focus away from the extraordinary but colorless plant life. But Mathers felt that we should emphasize the sea, the long stretch of backyard that led to it, and the existing light within the house. All these required day shots.

Mathers' solution was to air brush in the missing color, which resulted in a stunning cover featuring the afternoon sun bathing the back of the house, contrasted with the green of the lawn and shrubs and the blue of the pool.

One hardly noticed the leafless trees and the empty, dark flowerbeds.

The von Bülow family approved all the photographs and copy describing the property. In the end we produced a tasteful and non-invasive brochure that captured the emphasis on detail in the home and on the property without compromising the privacy of this famous family.

Power Marketing Begins

The brochure was sent to thousands of agents around the Northeast and as far away as Palm Beach, Washington, Beverly Hills, and other prominent agents nationally. It was also sent to our buyer mailing lists. The network evening news carried the story of Clarendon Court being brought to market, and the press covered it worldwide. Helicopters hovered overhead to show the house on the cliffs and the expanse of land. The story of the two trials, however, was recounted in the media *ad nauseum.*

Advertising was placed in all the major publications and timed to come out over the course of a month.

Given the notoriety and security issues, we did not have an open house in the traditional sense, but solicited the brokerage community so that they would feel part of the sale. We called high-profile agents directly; local and regional agents received a personalized letter inviting their cooperation. Anyone with a bona fide buyer would receive a private preview, and every agent making an inquiry received a detailed articulation of value.

Additionally, the rules of the process were made clear to all.

- The marketing campaign would go on until a specified date—some four weeks out.

- We would work with agents to set up the first showings—one hour each starting at 10 a.m. and ending at 3 p.m. on a date specified. We would continue until all buyers had their first showing.

- We would offer interested buyers a more extensive second showing, customized to their needs but within the 10 a.m. to 3 p.m. time frame. (We also indicated that second showings might occur with the representatives of others present, such as inspectors, contractors, financial counselors.)

- Every buyer and agent was told that we would set a time and date for all offers to be submitted in writing and delivered to our offices.

- All offers would have to make clear the contingencies, if any, and be accompanied by a good faith deposit of 10 percent of the offered price.

- The family would decide to whom they wanted to sell, for what price, and on what terms.

The Power Marketing Last Call

Our outreach on all fronts—locally, nationally, and internationally—worked. *Power marketing* was off and running as we began to fill the room. There were some fifteen requested and coordinated showings of the property, and every one of the potential buyers had been thoroughly vetted and deemed qualified. Chris Burr handled all the showings, while I worked the New York-based media. Five of the fifteen interested buyers arranged for second showings. Throughout, the showings were tightly organized and coordinated as much as possible to make sure everyone knew of everyone else's interest.

We then set the date, a Wednesday, for all bids to be in. How many buyers would actually bid on Clarendon Court caused much internal speculation. After first and second showings were completed, Burr called the buyers or their agents to inform them that we had fifteen potential bidders. In testimony to the power of making the last call, I learned later that, due to Burr's final call to the agents, one of the bidders increased his offer by $250,000. On the Wednesday deadline day, I was to come to the bank to meet with the children, their attorneys, and trust officers at 5 p.m. to present the bids and discuss them.

Suddenly Disaster

From Saturday to Wednesday I was alternatively elated at how well everything had gone and anxious about what the buyers would bid. On the appointed day there was an apprehensive quiet around our Park Avenue offices. All bids were due by 4:00 p.m.

By 3 p.m. nothing had arrived. At 3:30 p.m. the building's front desk rang my assistant, Sheila Johnson, asking her to come down because there were some people there with lots of equipment. She came back upstairs to inform me that there were two film crews waiting on the sidewalk for me to emerge with the bids.

At 4:01 p.m., however, with the deadline for offers officially behind us and none in hand, I now faced the prospect of being the orchestrator of a notorious real estate marketing failure. I saw my luxury marketing career going up in smoke and my firm's reputation tarnished—if not incinerated. The most celebrated sale of the decade was now turning into a disaster. And I was in the middle of it.

I took the men's room key and walked out into the corridor. As I passed the elevators, I saw a messenger with a helmet and cycling gloves waiting.

"Who are you waiting for?' I asked.

> The most celebrated sale of the decade was now turning into a disaster.

"I have a letter package for a David Mi-sha-now-ski or something like that."

"Give it to me," I demanded.

"My instructions are to wait until 4:10 p.m. to deliver it and it is only 4:05 now."

I grabbed the package out of his hand, ripped it open, and pulled out of the envelope a crisp one-page offer on fine linen stationery, elegantly signed with a fountain pen. There were no contingencies. The offer was for $4.2M cash, closing whenever the family desired. It was from a buyer and an agent that we knew were serious and credible.

"Yes!" I screamed. "Four point two. No contingencies. We have our buyer."

Our receptionist burst into tears. Everyone gathered around with a sigh of relief, knowing now that they had a job for at least a little while longer.

We called Don Fox to confirm that I would be there at 5 p.m. sharp. The front desk called again to say the reporters were blocking the entrance, and we needed to give them what they wanted or ask them to leave.

I put on my coat, tucked the offer into my briefcase, smiled, and gave everyone lots of pats on the back. I asked my assistant to call Borden and Burr. "Tell them the sun is shining in New York and in Newport."

Outside I stopped for the reporters. With cameras rolling and their microphones in my face, I simply said, "I have no comment on any aspect of the sale. If the family chooses to make an announcement it will come from them." I knew they would not likely find them. Safely in a taxi, I sped off to Rockefeller Center to meet with the family, their trust officers, and attorneys.

Delivering the Bid

Everyone gathered at the bank at 5 p.m. sharp. I again sat at the head of the long mahogany table.

"I have good news and bad news," I began. "The bad news is that we have only one offer. The good news is that it is for four point two million cash with no contingencies from a buyer who we have checked out. He is serious."

Relief swept over the room, followed by smiles and applause.

Clarendon Court closed in August of 1988 to a buyer from Washington, D.C. The buyer came through a referral to a local agent, Robin Corbin of Preferred Properties, from Edward Lee Cave, an esteemed broker in New York with an eponymous boutique firm. Throwing the net as far and as wide as possible and including everyone in the sale had worked.

> In testimony to the power of making the last call, one of the bidders increased his offer by $250,000.

An asking price articulated as a discount to core value had helped to achieve a record selling price in that market. It helped a very sophisticated buyer to appreciate that he was getting a bargain. Careful orchestration of the sale, especially the "last call," raised the comfort level higher to bid beyond the asking price, albeit within the valuation range we had defended.

In the end we had created a market for a property that many believed had none, and out of respect for the intelligence of the would-be buyers, we provided the threat of competition within that market so that someone was comfortable (and smart) enough to bid aggressively.

That December the buyer invited me to an event in New York, indicating that he wanted to give me a gift as a memento of his Clarendon Court purchase. I in turn asked him a question that had been bothering me. "Why did you have the messenger wait until 4:10 p.m. to present your offer?" His response was that he feared that there would be so many offers (read: competition) that he did not want his offer shopped to them by arriving too early.

The buyer's fear of potential competition confirmed that in the absence of multiple buyers the threat thereof was adequate enough to get a record price. It did not hurt that we also had a savvy buyer who was accustomed to paying up for things of quality.

An additional bid came in several days later, after the winner's had been accepted, offering "10 percent higher than the highest bid." The offer was rejected by the family and their attorneys because it came in late and they felt the offer may have been cleverly intended to dislodge the winning buyer, who had respected the rules. They feared that to consider a second offer after the first had been already accepted might result in so angering the first buyer that he might not sign a contract, leaving the family at the mercy of the second. Having eliminated the competition, the second buyer might then lower the price to be paid. Accordingly, the family went with the first buyer.

But the phrasing of the second belated offer was noteworthy. It was worded in a way also designed to overcome the threat of competition from all other bidders. *Power marketing* had worked again. The threat of competition produced multiple bids.

To this day, the first buyer is pleased with the record price he paid. More than twenty years later, he still lives in this magnificent property. I spoke with him while writing this book; he confirmed no regrets despite being the person who paid the extra $250,000. The threatened competition not only raised his comfort level to bid more, it also resulted in his winning the property.

The Takeaway _____

- Value was researched, determined, articulated, and then discounted to generate buyer interest.

- The room was filled by blanket offers of cooperation and compensation to agents everywhere and complemented by direct mail, advertising, and public relations marketing. The Champagne bottle was shaken vigorously.

- Multiplicity of interest was demonstrated to buyers through the staggered and tightly organized showings.

- Urgency to act was created by funneling interest to one moment in time when buyers would have to submit their bids.

- The last call provided a smart and highly sophisticated buyer the rationale needed to pay more than the asking price with delight and win the property.

- A second offer felt the threat of competition (and tried to eliminate it).

- The competitive threat of multiple buyers led the winner to engage in his own power play, instructing the messenger to wait until 4:10 p.m. to give him the last word.

9

Business Essentials of a Luxury Listing Contract

When listing a mass market property, you probably run to your file drawer or MLS site and pull out the basic three- or six-month listing agreement provided by your local board of Realtors®. In some cases, however, this listing agreement is not geared to the luxury market. If you use an agreement not tailored to the differences in the luxury market, you risk seriously shortchanging yourself.

In this chapter, I outline the essentials of a luxury listing agreement framed so that both seller and agent can arrive at fair and mutually beneficial terms.[23]

Review Every Sentence with the Client

At the end of listing appointments (if I want to list the property), I go over the listing contract right there, line by line. While surely some clients find this tedious, most come away impressed with the seriousness with which I take the contract and the expertise demonstrated through this review. In turn, the client takes the agreement more seriously, too. While I always encourage sellers to have a lawyer go over the listing agreement, my review of the contract with the clients often allows them to answer their own lawyer's objections. The listing terms on my website have withstood hundreds of such objections. After customization by a lawyer, a listing contract that embodies them should protect you and your client, and provide the foundation for a solid relationship.

About Risk

The listing contract is designed to reduce some of the risk that you and your client are taking regarding the listing and sale of such a valuable asset with such a large commission (as I will argue later, the commission should be large). It also aims to create a fair balance between both sides.

Chapter 2 demonstrated the smallness of the luxury market and warned that this presents formidable risks. To review:

- The risk from being on the market longer. Because most luxury properties take at least twelve to sixteen months to sell (in reasonably good markets), the minimum term of the agreement must be the average time luxury properties are on the market or longer. Don't risk losing the sale because of a shorter agreement.

- The risk associated with spending more money. You will spend more money on marketing a luxury property, most of which will be spent upfront in the initial two or three months of the listing.

- The risk from spending more time. *Power marketing* techniques require more time to create the optimal conditions for the sale. You must be personally present for showings, update sellers more frequently, and coordinate a team of accountants, lawyers, trust officers, investment advisors, public relations people, etc.

Your compensation needs to account for these risks through an increased commission (see Chapter 11), greater protection in the listing agreement, or both.

Greater Expertise Needed

Moreover, what you do as a power marketer requires not just more time and money, but also greater expertise. Your sales strategy and activities are fundamentally different from, and more substantial than what they are for ordinary sales. Creating a market for a property that is normally created by the MLS demands an expertise few have and, therefore, deserves greater compensation.

Be Unafraid to Talk About It

As previously noted, luxury property owners are successful business people who did not become rich by needlessly risking money or time on anything. They understand risk and reward and appreciate your discussing it openly with them. But if they are not made conscious of the compensation you need for undertaking greater risk, they will, like any good business person, bargain for the best terms possible.

Furthermore, haphazard negotiations over the listing agreement often foreshadow problems down the line. Whenever I have seen a luxury owner negotiate a listing agreement that offers weak protection for the hired agency, disaster usually looms not far ahead, for the agent and the homeowner. Why? Because the homeowner has struck a fundamentally unfair deal with the agency. That, in turn, can lead to either bitterness between the parties or a less than zealous effort by the agent.

> The industry's reputation is hurt by not asking for compensation and protection equal to the risk, expertise and time required for luxury brokerage.

Luxury homeowners know that a good listing contract provides a strong foundation for a successful business transaction. The industry's reputation is hurt by not asking for compensation and protection equal to the risk, expertise and time required for luxury brokerage. Most luxury owners will understand and agree to these terms—so don't be afraid to ask for them.

Creating Your Stance

From the outset, your stance must be that of an agent with high standards and solid business practices who will not take undue risk, but can provide substantial marketing rewards for your client. You must state what you need in order to deliver what they need. Remember, the sellers are focused on their rewards (a sale) and not on your risks. Having included all the following provisions into my listing contracts for many years, I know they are not difficult to obtain or explain. Nor are they unreasonable. If done properly, discussing them will solidify your relationship with the sellers and their attorneys from the beginning.

ABOUT INVOLVING ATTORNEYS

Far too often, we see the attorney as necessary only at the end of the process, more for cleanup than for strategy or negotiating. This is a mistake. Lawyers should be brought in at the beginning of the process, preferably during the listing contract negotiation. The owners may hesitate, not wanting the legal meter running, but explain to them that it will prevent problems from surfacing during the marketing, bidding, and sales process.

Dealing with a client's attorney can be daunting; therefore, it's important to know what to expect and how to handle him from the start.

An attorney's job is to protect his client. He spends all day negotiating, battling with other attorneys over contracts, terms, assets, and even property. Know in advance that when presented with the listing contract, he may trash it and replace it with his own. By providing your agreement first, you have established your ground rules; now, he must establish his. All of this is just posturing, but it is his job to butt heads with you right up front. Expect it.

It is also his wish to get the property listed and sold for his client—he does not want to become an impediment to the sale. Furthermore, he would rather list with an agent who provides clear explanations and a negotiating stance. When you demonstrate your negotiating acumen right from the start with the listing agreement, the lawyer is more likely to respect you enough to put his client in your hands.

Gaining Respect

In fact, butting heads with attorneys can serve you well in the long run. Oftentimes, the attorneys I negotiate with the hardest are the ones that refer me to other clients and attorneys later on. The tougher the negotiations and my position, the more respect and business I earn. A good friend of mine, Bob Baraf of Cushman and Wakefield, similarly earned an exclusive leasing assignment for one of the most prestigious office buildings in Manhattan that paid him millions in commissions yearly, all from the respect he acquired from the other side's attorney. That attorney came away from the negotiation with Bob recommending that his client hire him for their side.

Earning the attorney's respect is also important at other moments in the sale, like when making definitive recommendations for a price adjustment, or dealing with problems that will inevitably surface, or accepting an offer that you believe will not be bettered.

To repeat: don't view the attorney as someone invited only at the end of the marketing process, like a guest invited only after the party ends to assist in cleanup. Invite the lawyer right from the start. Keep him involved through all aspects of the process—marketing plans, showings, offers (or lack thereof), and any movements in the marketplace. Doing so will ensure the deal goes more smoothly and puts you on equal footing with someone who should be your partner in executing and reaching the goals of your mutual principal.

Twelve Essential Business Principles of a Good Luxury Listing Contract

1. Enabling Clauses

Usually listing agreements begin with the granting or "enabling" clauses under which the owner(s) grant the exclusive right to sell their property. The listing agreement authorizes (or enables) you to offer the property at the listed price, normally some dollar amount payable in cash or other terms acceptable to the seller. This section also deals with terms and effective date(s).

Additionally, these clauses enable you to do certain things, such as market the property, use sub-agents or buyer brokers, advertise, create brochures, hold open houses, put up signs, use the MLS, list the property on the Internet, and so on. This is all somewhat boilerplate. However, one clause is quite important: that the owner will refer all inquiries or offers concerning the listed property to you.

This sentence provides an important protection for you, the agent. It gets to the heart of an exclusive right to sell listing (which I recommend), and it is what makes it different from an exclusive agency listing (which I strongly discourage).

This clause removes the risk that a neighbor or friend will bypass you by negotiating a deal directly with the owner. It obligates the owner to refer all inquiries or offers concerning the listed property to you; anything else violates the terms of the contract. More seriously, to do otherwise might even be construed as conspiracy to defraud on the part of both the owner and her friends or neighbors. This accusation is grave and carries serious legal ramifications in many states, including treble damages in some.

I have heard some agents argue that as long as they have an exclusive right to sell listing, why should they care if the owner negotiates her own deal with a buyer? After all, the exclusive right to sell means the agent still gets paid.

There are many reasons not to do this, including:

- The seller will feel you did not do your job.

- You may have breached your fiduciary duty to the seller.

- If the buyer decides against purchase, you will lose someone who might buy another property.

- You will become known as the agent who collected a commission for doing nothing, not good word-of-mouth marketing.

- You have violated the fundamental goal of all *power marketing*—to get multiple buyers bidding simultaneously on a property.

2. Getting Paid: How and When?

The following clause is one of the most important in the listing agreement. You should know it well and be able to negotiate it at the drop of a hat.

The clause says that if during the term of the contract the listed property is sold or the broker or anyone else (including but not limited to a buyer's broker) finds a buyer ready, willing, and able to buy the listed property on the terms specified in this contract or on any other terms acceptable to the owners, he will pay the broker a commission of some percent of the agreed upon sales price at time of closing or at time of default, whichever comes sooner.

This clause varies according to state laws, so it's important to consult an attorney. In New York, for instance, agents can be paid for finding a "ready, willing, and able buyer" who agrees to the listing price or any terms acceptable to the seller.

As discussed in Chapter 4, listing prices are meant to generate interest and provide a target for buyers. But they are almost always aggressive, educated guesses of what a property is likely to fetch. This clause says that if you get the seller the listed price, aggressive as it may be, you should be paid. You may indeed strive for more than the listed price (and should), but in the end, if you hit that price, you are due your commission.

This clause gets to the heart of the business transaction. I don't work for anyone who does not hire me, which means I don't work on open listings. When hired, I want to know both how much I am getting paid and what I have to do to earn it. Hitting the asking price and the stated terms of the listing, as with *Le Domaine Résistance*, is earning my commission.

The likelihood of getting the asking price for a luxury property is often slim at the outset. Therefore, if an owner is reluctant or unwilling to pay someone for getting what is often an aggressive price, then how will she feel about getting less, the scenario you face most of the time?

This clause also gets to the heart of seller motivation. If the seller is not willing to pay for success, then why are you talking to her at all? Avoid sellers who waste your time. By discussing this clause with the seller, you can ascertain whether she is worth your time and investment.

Set the Terms

Price is not the only factor in a sale; the terms also are important. You may bring in a full price offer, but it might require, for instance, 100 percent seller financing or a one-year closing, or it may include other terms unacceptable to the seller.

Put in the listing agreement under "terms" any that are appropriate. For instance you could write, "Terms: cash, no contingencies, closing within sixty days or less."

Work with the seller's lawyer to determine exactly under what circumstance or terms you will be paid. Those circumstances should be made crystal clear so that there is no question about when, why, or how much commission is due or what you must do to earn it. When I am clearly focused on my target, I find it easier to hit it.

3. Buyer Default Clause

The buyer default clause says that should the buyer default in the performance of the contract, the broker will be entitled, in lieu of commission, to no more than one-half of any deposits forfeited by the buyer. As a consequence of any buyer default, the seller is going to get as much as a 10 percent windfall, which was brought about by you. This clause says that you are entitled to a portion of that money because you found a buyer, negotiated up to a price acceptable to the seller, and got him into contract. I propose settling for one-half the deposit. This is fair because you and the seller have both been inconvenienced by the default.

Half the Deposit versus Half the Retained Deposit

Attorneys sometimes argue that brokers should get one-half of any "retained" deposits. I tend to go along with this argument—with a little foot dragging—because I am sympathetic to a situation in which an owner has to go into her own pocket (on a $3M sale that would be a couple hundred thousand dollars) to pay me. By agreeing to keep a portion of any retained deposit, you protect the client from having to do this. Remember, however, that if the buyer defaults and the seller chooses not to retain the deposit, you get nothing.

If for some reason you cannot get one-half the deposit, then at an absolute minimum you should get your commission percentage multiplied by the defaulted amount, i.e., 6 percent times the 10 percent deposit. This means that if the default amount is $300,000 on a $3M sale, then, at a minimum, you should get the commission times that amount, or $18,000.

Failed sale	$3,000,000
Default amount	$300,000 (10 percent)
Multiplied by your commission	6 percent
Minimum payment	$18,000

While this is the minimum you should accept, do not concede this too quickly. Argue for 50 percent and only grudgingly drop back to 25 percent, and then 10 percent, and finally the amount of your commission only as a last resort. I have yet to find an attorney who isn't willing to give me my commission on the defaulted amount and allow his client to retain the difference, but that is far too generous to the other side. By agreeing to pay your percentage commission times the retained defaulted amount, you don't get much, but at least some money was extracted out of this bad situation.

Split What Is Received on Default?

Please note that there is nothing that says you have to split the money received upon a default with the selling broker. If that agent were in my firm, I might. If not, I would not. It is incumbent upon the buyer broker to think through the possibility that her buyer may default and thus get a default clause into her buyer brokerage agreement. If she does, she is covered by her agreement and you are covered by yours. As an additional benefit, by putting the responsibility on the buyer agent for collecting her piece of any retained deposit, you serve the seller better by decreasing the chances of a buyer default. This is because if the buyer does default, she would not only lose her deposit but, in addition, would have to pay her buyer agent—a double whammy.

Getting the Listing Extended

If you grant the concession of being paid only your percentage commission on the defaulted amount, make sure you get something in return, such as an extension of the listing agreement for a time equal to the period from signed contract to time of default. This allows you more time to recover your investment by extending your exclusive right to sell. I encourage the inclusion of the following.

> *Should the Buyer default in the performance of the contract, the agent will be entitled, in lieu of commission, to no more than one-half of any deposits given by the Buyer and retained by the Seller, and this listing contract will be extended for a period of time equal to that from date of contract to the date of default.*

Most attorneys do not have any problem allowing an extended chance to sell the property, since a default is not something a broker can control. The seller wants the property sold anyway and has already decided on you. So extending the listing should not be an issue.

4. Owner Default Clause

Next you must address what happens if the owner defaults. A typical default clause says that should the owner default in the performance of the contract, then the commission is earned, due, and payable in full at the time of such default.

If you found someone acceptable to the owner who then entered into a contract and the owner failed to perform, you should not be penalized in any way. There is no excuse for not being paid if the seller defaults. On this point, too, I have yet to find an attorney who would not agree.

5. Withdrawal Clause

A withdrawal clause has to do with the possibility that an owner's circumstances may change, leading to a decision to withdraw the property from the market. Given the enormous amount of money and time spent on a luxury property, it can be a significant problem in luxury real estate. I try to have the discussion of this clause revolve around two principles:

Principle #1: The seller can withdraw from the market at any time, but I must be compensated at least for out-of-pocket expenses and time invested.

Principle #2: If the seller withdraws, they cannot then sell the property themselves or through another broker during the period of the original listing agreement without paying me the full commission.

The second principle means that the terms of the listing agreement are still alive after a withdrawal, but are applied only in the event of a sale by the owner. This means that if the client has bona fide reasons to withdraw and there will be no sale, then the seller can pay the amounts negotiated in Principle #1 and be done. But if the seller is trying to circumvent paying a commission by using the withdrawal clause, the broker is protected.

The clause I use states that should the owner withdraw this property from the market before the listing expiration date, then the owner will pay me, within thirty days of such action, all documented marketing expenses to include photography, brochure preparation, and production, mailings, advertising, and other promotional expenses specific to the property. In addition, in consideration of the time and overhead associated with marketing the property, a fee of 1 percent of the listed price is due. I also note that a withdrawal "shall not be construed as releasing the owner(s) from any other provisions of this agreement."

Because withdrawal does not release the owners from the agreement, if they sell the property during the term of the agreement, they owe a commission. This is an important sentence because owners could lie about their reasons for withdrawal to save a commission and then turn around and sell it themselves. Without this clause you are not protected from this eventuality.

I have sometimes encountered the following objection: What if Mr. and Mrs. Seller were to die and their heirs decided not to sell the house? Why should they be penalized by having to pay your expenses and a 1 percent fee for something beyond their control?

My first response to this is, if they should not be penalized for circumstances outside their control, why should I? If a consumer hires a contractor to put a new addition onto her house and dies, should the contractor not be paid? What about the contractor's loss of revenue and opportunity from working on this job instead of working on another? What about the time investment and out-of-pocket expenses that were incurred? Is he to absorb the loss? Like a contractor, I need compensation for the time and money invested.

In addition, I remind the attorney that clearly the owner's wishes were to sell the house. After all, that is why the heirs are talking to me. If it is the choice of the heirs not to comply with the wishes of the owners, why should I be penalized for their decision?

If the situation is not the extreme of death but rather the owner asking what happens if he changes his mind, I ask the following question: *"Perhaps you could tell me what you think are the chances of your withdrawing the property?"* Then pause and listen.

> I need compensation for the time and money invested.

If I do not get a satisfactory response, I probe further. *"Is there anything I should know now about your circumstances that would prompt such a withdrawal?"* Do not speak until they do.

If they say, *"No, absolutely not. There is nothing we are aware of,"* then I say, *"Great, then we should not be worried about the penalties of a withdrawal because it is not likely to occur."* But if they start telling me about the circumstances under which a withdrawal could happen, then I must evaluate what they say and decide if I want an assignment that carries the risk.

Whatever is said, I like to remind the clients that I am investing a substantial amount of money, talent and time in their sale. I cannot commit to them unless they are prepared to commit to me.

A Question of Quality

The most valid rationale for a withdrawal has nothing to do with external circumstances but rather a case in which an agent performs poorly. If you are a good luxury marketer, there is an easy answer. My response is:

> *I come highly recommended. You have seen my letters of reference, my testimonials, and my track record. I have given you a copy of the marketing plan for your property. There is no question about what I am going to do and when I am going to do it. The only things left are matters of my diligence and negotiating ability and whether we can all get along together. If you are not sure, please ask me anything you wish before we proceed. This is important for both of us.*

The withdrawal clause discussion is about the real possibility of the seller withdrawing and a theoretical discussion about his withdrawing. If there is a real possibility, you have to flush it out now. The theoretical discussion helps understand his motivation to sell, and what could prompt him not to sell. That is why this clause is so helpful. It protects you and prompts discussion that helps you decide If you can work with the sellers.

6. Reasonable Legal Fees

This clause means that if you have to sue the owner for a commission, she pays the legal tab. You may want to leave out the word "reasonable" in your draft agreement so that her attorney can put it in, feeling that he has left a mark on the agreement. You should not have much trouble inserting this clause unless she really does not intend to pay (in which case she will give you a lot of trouble). But at least you were forewarned.

7. Protection Clause

After filling in the date of expiration, it is important to put into the contract a clause that protects you for a commission after the expiration of the contract if the property is purchased by any buyers who saw it during your term as agent. My clause reads as follows:

> *This Agreement shall expire on _____.*
> *Notwithstanding such expiration, I shall be entitled to a commission if after such date the Owner(s) sells the property or any portion thereof (1) to any Buyer with whom negotiations were pending at the time of such expiration or (2) within twelve months of such expiration to any Buyer to whom the Property was shown by me or any other broker through whom I marketed the Property. I will submit a list to the Owner(s) of all known protected buyers under (1) and (2) above, within fourteen days of the expiration of the listing agreement.*

This clause is particularly important given the nature of the luxury buyers with whom you are dealing—buyers who do not have to buy and who, therefore, have a diminished urgency to act. Luxury buyers get easily distracted. They might have a new merger to handle or a new film to produce. Buying their dream home can often take a back seat to more pressing business.

This all means that a buyer who views the property during its initial week on the market may come back months or even a year later to buy. You must protect yourself against this eventuality. After all, the seller hired you to find buyers; if you find those buyers during your tenure as listing broker, you should not be penalized if they decide to buy the day after the listing expires.

Seasoned agents know that buyers can often sense a listing expiration on the horizon. They may delay their negotiations in the hope that after the listing expires they can get the property at a discount. It is also true that agents who neglect to include the protection clause start to panic about sixty days before their listing expires. The volume and intensity of calls to buyers will increase substantially during this period. Many a broker will unwittingly call buyers with the subliminal message, "Hurry and buy this because my list-ing is running out." Buyers can sense a squeeze coming.

> Agents who neglect to include the protection clause start to panic about sixty days before their listing expires.

This won't happen if you have a protection clause. Rather, your pro-fessionalism will remain intact and your calm demeanor will better serve the seller.

Only rarely have I encountered problems with a protection clause from an attorney. The principal point of debate is whether the broker should have twelve months or less. I can settle for nine, but not less than six. I worked hard for all those buyers; I have no intention of handing them over to the seller without an obligation to pay.

The protection clause also serves another purpose: protecting other agents. Because of it I can protect them for a commission six to twelve months after the listing expires. This raises their comfort level in deal-ing with me because they know they will get paid if I register the name of their buyer with the seller upon expiration. This kind of clause is particularly important thirty to sixty days before an expiration, as the other agents feel a high comfort level in still bringing their buyer to the situation, knowing they are protected.

8. Lease Protection Clause

If you operate in a resort area or a location where there is a high likeli-hood of the seller renting the property during the term of the listing, you should know about the lease protection clause. It protects you against an interruption of marketing due to a seller leasing the property. The clause consists of an agreement to extend the period of the listing by a time equivalent to the term of any lease. My clause reads as follows:

> *Should the Owner(s) lease the Listed Property during the above listing period, this agreement will be automatically extended for a period equal to the term of the lease.*

When I worked the Hamptons, sellers were attracted to the pos-sibility of renting their home for the summer months, as rentals could fetch hefty prices. Often after listing their property, they would inform me in May that they had "just" secured an irresistible summer rental. They would assure me not to worry because the tenants would allow it to be shown on twenty-four-hour notice.

This is an agent's nightmare, not only because the casualness of the vacation season makes it difficult to show a property looking its best, but also because buyers expect immediate showings in resort areas. They will drop into a local broker's office on one of their vacation afternoons and want to see a property right then. The renters, however, who are responsible for how the property looks are, after all, on vacation. That means they often leave a house untidy. Even after giving the tenant twenty-four-hour notice, it's not uncommon to find snorkels in the hall, wet towels on the floor, or last night's pizza still on the counter. This poor showing radically reduces the chances of a sale. Thus, even with a twenty-four-hour notice built into the lease, renters are a problem.

> Even after giving the tenant twenty-four-hour notice, it's not uncommon to find snorkels in the hall, wet towels on the floor, or last night's pizza still on the counter.

The lease protection clause can protect you from such situations. It can, in effect, provide you with two selling seasons. In the Hamptons, for instance, the traditional listing period was January and February, and the traditional selling season was February through May 1 (so people could get in by Memorial Day and enjoy the season). If a listing did not sell by May 1, sellers would turn to the rental market. By renting out their home for three months, the lease protection clause extends your listing for three months, which means that in the case of a year listing agreement expiring in February, the listing would extend until May of the following year, thus giving you two selling seasons. Adapt this to your local conditions.

9. Bind Those Who Come After

If anyone dies, make sure the agreement does not die with them. You want to be the listing broker for the seller's heirs, or for the estate, and you want the executor bound by this agreement. If the seller were to die, there is sometimes a new urgency to act, often for estate tax purposes. Make sure that you are in the picture should this unfortunate situation occur.

I use a clause like this:

"This Agreement shall be binding upon and inure to the benefit of the respective executors, administrators, heirs, successors and assigns of the parties...."

This clause also protects against a seller assigning the property to others, willingly or unwillingly (as per "assigns" in the clause above). If, for instance, the client goes into bankruptcy, you should be protected because the property will be assigned to a bankruptcy estate and will be administrated by a bankruptcy trustee. You can then continue trying to sell it for the bankruptcy estate.

10. Warranty Clause

The warranty clause simply warrants that the title is marketable and that the undersigned have the right to sell the property. This is useful for large landed tracts where title can get fuzzy, or in water-oriented properties where erosion or accretion or high water lines make for title issues. Most lawyers and owners do not object to this. If anything, it forces the lawyers to be sure that all is fine with the title before selling commences, rather than after. My clause reads:

"The undersigned warrants that they are the sole owner of the property, that title is marketable, and that they have the right to sell the property."

11. Exclusion Clause

Sometimes sellers want to exclude certain buyers from the listing agreement. You already know that you cannot get the highest price for your seller without creating a competitive situation and that such exclusions give these potential buyers a preferential position in the negotiations. That discourages others from bidding. Thus, avoid such clauses.

> The best way to handle the request for an exclusion is to agree to it, but with a narrow window for the buyer to act.

Overcome the Objection by Agreeing to It

Surprisingly, the best way to handle the request for an exclusion is to agree to it, but with a narrow window for the buyer to act. If this issue comes up, add to the listing agreement an exclusion clause that allows fourteen days for the seller to try to make a deal with a list of excluded buyers, which you then attach to the agreement. Have the seller sign the normal agreement with this clause included. Then, once signed, let the sellers indulge their desire to try to make that deal.

If, as is most likely, the sellers cannot come to a deal, then the listing commences and there are no exclusions. If anyone from that list purchases after the exclusion period, you get paid because you got them to do something the seller could not. You also might pick up a few buyers or at least some contacts.

In Deed

Reading deeds should be a part of your regular homework. Ask the attorney or the owner for a copy of the deed and read it before taking the listing—not after. After a few deeds, you'll be able to quickly recognize red flag items, such as easements, exclusions, mineral rights, rights of way, imprecise boundary descriptions, and so on.

12. Get a Lawyer Clause

My last clause is boilerplate text:

"This is a legally binding contract. If not understood, seek competent legal advice."

There are other things the lawyers may insist upon, such as including the marketing plan as part of the legal agreement. Since you intend on creating a marketing plan (and hopefully already have), you should have no problem agreeing to incorporate it. The lawyer may also want you to warrant that you will screen the financial capability of buyers, which you should do routinely, so agree to it. To purchase a winning Marketing Plan as a master for all your listings, go to ***http://PowerMarketing.pro*** under "Buy". Agents have been delighted with the successful response this plan gets from consumers.

The Takeaway

- Spend time creating a contract that compensates you for the risks inherent in the luxury market.

- Involve the attorneys from the beginning. Make them comfortable with your position, experience and marketing plan. They will become your allies, and sometimes even a business referral.

- Set the terms and clauses appropriate for your time and money investment.

- Protect yourself and your time from a buyer or owner default or withdrawals with the appropriate deposits or fees due you in case the transaction is not completed.

- Review every line of the contract with your client. Similarly, read all deeds and other related documents.

- Allow exclusions only if absolutely necessary, but then do your sellers a favor by forcing them to act within a narrow time frame.

10

For Sale by Owner (FSBO)

Working with a FSBO offers great practice in objection handling and lead generation, as well as providing an opportunity to improve your success with listing appointments. If nothing else, this practice allows you to fine tune your skills with no downside risk.

A FSBO luxury homeowner is after all another high-end contact. Whether you want her listing or not, working with her may propel your business into the right circles. Moreover, there is more than an 85 percent chance that the FSBO will end up hiring an agent to sell her home. Working with her now positions you for that possibility later.

Finally, if you do decide to take the listing later, it is likely the property has not sold because it was overpriced, has been made stale by the owner's attempt, or has just been sitting too long on the market. Now, you should be able to list it more realistically and possibly secure a well-priced listing with a more motivated seller. You may even be able to engage in stepladder marketing, as demonstrated in the example of *Le Domaine Résistance.*

You also may be able to position the property in the market at a discount from the value it might have gotten earlier. As you now know, offering a luxury property at a discount is an easier sale to our sophisticated buyers, especially if markets have improved during the time the FSBO was trying to sell it herself.

Why People Become FSBOs

In order to deal with FSBOs, let's review why some luxury homeowners decide to go this route. You want to know all the reasons so that you can adapt the listing presentation to meet them.

1   They see buyers everywhere with properties selling quickly and sense the market is strong and therefore believe they don't need an agent.
2   They believe selling their property will be easy.
3   Because of the active market and the ease of selling, they want to save a commission.
4   They have the time to do their own marketing, showing, and negotiating.
5   They secretly have always wanted to be real estate agents. This is their chance.
6   They think they know the potential buyer. Their neighbor or friends, for instance, may have expressed an interest in the property, and they think these people will now buy it. They may also feel that they know all the potential buyers for their property because of their social or geographic relationships—they play or live in the same places. Indeed, of the 11 percent of sellers who sell their homes without using a real estate agent, about 37 percent sell it to someone they have known.[24]
7   They have not found an agent that they think is competent. This is where your opportunity lies.

At the core, however, they become FSBOs because they do not understand the expertise and skill involved in what a luxury broker does. They think advertising works and open houses are simple exercises rather than highly coordinated tools to influence how the brokerage community views the listing. They don't practice objection handling at open houses because they cannot imagine any objection to their home. They know nothing about positively controlling the psychology of the sale because they know of no reason to be negative. They confuse securing buyers with knowing what to do with them. They think they only need one buyer and don't understand the importance of two or just the threat of two. They care about getting their price without understanding that marketing, not the seller, sets the price. So forgive them.

CONTROLLING YOUR ATTITUDE TOWARD FSBOS

Let's deal with the possibility that you take umbrage at a FSBO because you resent their assumption that selling a home is easy.

I know how you feel. I feel the same way, but what I have found is that everyone has a right to maximize the amount of money that they get from the sale of one of their largest assets. I take my role to be that of their real estate financial counselor. If I really thought they could make more money by selling it themselves, I would recommend telling them that. They may still hire me to be an intermediary and handle the negotiations.

Think of this benefit. Sometimes the victory is not a sale as much as it is the contact or new relationship that will generate future business. If I do negotiate the sale, it is one more to tuck under my belt. If, by chance, it is a very expensive or prestigious sale, then I want even more to be involved.

I like to approach FSBOs with understanding and respect for their desire to save money, because I believe in most cases they have just not found an agent to whom they are willing to entrust the sale. If they did, I think they would be more likely to pay a commission. Because it is highly likely the FSBO will fail in their attempt to sell themselves, when they do so and are in need of an agent, I want to be the first person they turn to. They will do so, if my attitude shows empathy and understanding for what they were attempting to do and if I provide quality consultative advice. My confident assumption is that if I can explain to them how I can help them through my *power marketing*, they will have found the agent they seek in me.

Helping a FSBO

If you accept my rationale of relationship building as the primary reason for helping a FSBO, then how should you go about doing so? The National Association of Realtors® has provided a useful checklist.[25] It's not completely applicable to the luxury market, but it's a good start.

- Advise on how to get the house ready for sale.

- Provide information on how they can obtain lead paint disclosure packets from HUD.

- Give them a list of other property disclosure forms.

- Make a list of inspections often required of the seller, such as a home inspection, termite inspection, radon report, as well as a list of all condominium or cooperative documents and HOA or co-op board application forms.

- Give them a blank seller and buyer net sheet to calculate what they will realize from the sale.

- Inform them of the various means of exposure and advertising, including the MLS, listing firms like Help U Sell, discount brokerage firms, websites such as For Sale by Owner.com.

- Provide suggestions for print ads, signs, open house teepees, sign-in sheets, etc.

> Being grouped with others on mass Do It Yourself (DIY) websites may drive FSBOs back to you—and quickly.

- Tell them how you qualify buyers and give them a buyer qualification form.

- Give them a copy of the HUD Settlement Sheet (leave blank).

- Provide an overview of mortgage financing, if applicable.

- Give them school reports for their buyers, if applicable.

- Give them some tips on staging for their open house.

- Tell them how you would show the property.

How to Change the FSBO's Mind

- Elaborate upon the complexities of the open house and that the owner, being self interested, cannot conduct it the way an independent third party with credibility in the brokerage community can.

- Explain that there is a better than 90 percent chance that the buyer is already sitting in the brokerage community.

- Explain how the open house is a way to positively influence the psychology of the agents and the buyers they represent, as we've discussed in Chapter 6. This gives you an opportunity to demonstrate your *power marketing* expertise and maybe get the listing signed right there.

- Engage them in a discussion of pricing. Let them tell you how they arrived at it.
- Explain how pricing is a function of marketing and how FSBO sites lead to discount pricing, not pricing to get the highest amount.
- Speak to them about safety issues. If the sellers are not utilizing the brokerage community, then they are opening up their property to the general public with no filter or intermediary as a buffer. Public open houses risk attracting those who are interested in something other than buying a property.
- The FSBO's most effective marketing tool is the yard sign. But yard signs work best in high-traffic locations, which most luxury neighborhoods are not. Moreover, using one can cheapen the property, reducing its cachet, thereby working against the sale.

10 packs of my booklet for consumers, *"Getting the Highest Price: Power Marketing for Luxury Homeowners,"* can be bought at *http://PowerMarketing.pro*. For a modest investment, you can show FSBOs how to get the highest price and learn the marketing techniques needed to sell. By giving them the booklet, you may also clinch a multi-million dollar listing.

So if a FSBO wishes to under-price a property, then as I mentioned earlier, direct them to one of the many discount brokerage firms that for a flat fee provide some of the services needed. For example, FSBOs who spend $600 with a firm in Utah get a yard sign, a listing on the company's website and on MLS, all the forms they will need, a booklet on selling and marketing (they should give them the book above), and disclosure forms. For an additional 1 percent, an agent will write the offer, review the documentation, and attend the closing. What they do not get is pricing guidance, advertising, caravan tour attention, and, perhaps most importantly, a practitioner with whom to strategize, let alone orchestrate the sale.

By putting the property on the MLS, these listing firms may expose the seller to a commission for the buyer broker, requiring them to pay at least half what they would traditionally have paid. This is because the biggest complaint from buyer agents where there is no listing broker is that they do the work of the listing and the buying agent. Therefore, when they see that the listing agent is a discounter, they sometimes expect a higher commission for doing double work. Apprise the clients that they may have to deal with this objection and, as a consequence, raise the amount of commission offered to the buying agent. Already one can see the commission rising from 2.5 percent up to 3.5 percent, 4 percent, or higher.

MAKE YOUR POINT

It doesn't hurt to leave the FSBO with these quick points:

- Without the benefit of *power marketing*, luxury FSBOs are left with discount pricing as the primary lure. They may never know the true price they could have gotten.

- They deny themselves access to where the buyers are: in the brokerage community.

- They deny themselves professional marketing that creates a market and an urgency for buyers to participate in it.

- FSBOs require lots of advertising because it is both their primary tool and the least effective.

- Almost nine out of ten FSBOs end up using an agent anyway, pay a commission, but still get a lower price because the property's prime marketing period was wasted.

- People who use an agent, sell their home for about 15 percent more than people who sell their homes themselves.[26]

Yet another reason no one should be a FSBO is that NAR studies have found that the number of weeks on the market will be longer.[27] If the property is on the market longer, it is more likely to get stale and will have dissipated the initial urgency to act that comes from buyers' fear that it will sell quickly. Once that initial period passes, their fear of loss quickly turns into a belief that no one wants the property, as seen with *Le Domaine Résistance.*

In sum, discount brokerages provide FSBOs with some of the forms, processes, and procedures they need, but none of the expertise required for *power marketing.* I would always recommend that such discounted marketing methods be avoided. But if the sellers insist on using them, at least provide them with some direction.

SELLER BEWARE

Not only are sellers likely to get a lower price, but they may not save on the commission after all. Why? Because buyers know all about real estate commissions, and they automatically assume that they can discount a luxury FSBO price by the amount of the commission. Therefore, only the buyer, not the seller, saves a commission on the FSBO sale.

Because it is highly unlikely that any FSBO can orchestrate multiple buyers all bidding simultaneously, the buyers will lack urgency. Luxury FSBOs have exposed themselves to buyers who are smart, sophisticated, and intelligent—and will use the lack of competition to get a bargain instead.

The Takeaway

- Provide luxury FSBOs with information, establish a relationship as a helpful adviser, and position yourself as a reliable agent.

- Because luxury FSBO listings stay on the market longer, involve greater inconvenience and safety issues and rely on discounting to attract buyers, they result in either a lower sales price or the sellers end up listing with an agent anyway, usually at less than might originally have been achieved.

- The luxury FSBO "challenge" is a perfect opportunity to practice and improve your *power marketing* skill.

11

Getting a Higher Commission and Why You Should

A good real estate listing agent should be an essential member of every affluent person's financial team, together with a trust officer, a stock broker or investment adviser, a lawyer, a tax attorney, and, if applicable, a property manager. Unlike with other team members, an agent's compensation is usually based upon a success fee—in other words, commission. Commissions are not fixed; they are negotiable.[28] That means they can go down, and up.

The less you charge, the less people will think of you. Think of yourself as a value-added marketing consultant. You have to value the service you provide in line with the benefit and added dollars you create. If you have grasped the *power marketing* lessons of this book and combined them with local market knowledge, then you are now a "leading authority" on selling property in your market. There are almost 3 million licensed agents out there (a little over 1 million belong to NAR); you represent but a fraction of those agents who spend on themselves to buy a book or tapes to improve and learn. You are a rarity. The information you have now is virtually unknown to others and thus not widely practiced. You should never balk at charging a considerable fee for it, because when implemented it adds value and dollars for your client.

My former firm charged a 10 percent commission on listings, as did most of our competitors in the luxury business back then.

This was a bargain, as confirmed by a Goldman Sachs banker who had received one of my mailings around bonus time and asked me to come to his office to pitch him on selling his home in Southampton, New York.

When I arrived, I knew I was in trouble when his secretary asked me if I was his 3:05 appointment. *"No,"* I replied. *"My appointment was for 3 p.m." "Oh, yes,"* she said.

It seemed that my appointment time was limited to five minutes. Everything got worse when I entered this high-powered potential client's office.

"You have 90 seconds to tell me what I need to know, after which I will tell you if you have the assignment." he said.

Clearly, I was dealing with a "driver" personality type who was willing to listen—for a minute and a half.

Obviously, there was little time for questions or dialogue, so my presentation went something like this.[29]

"What I do is not for everyone. My firm is one of the most expensive real estate brokerage firms in the market. We charge a premium 10 percent commission for a premium service. We do not take an upfront fee and we risk our capital and time. We only take an exclusive right to sell listing for a minimum of one year.

"If we take your listing there is a 93 percent chance that we will get it sold. That is our historical track record. My personal track record [I handed him a list of all the properties I had sold] is the same. I can provide you references from the 93 percent for whom I succeeded and the 7 percent for whom I did not.

"To achieve this success, I employ the following strategy: the goal of everything I do is to get you to one moment in time when you will have multiple buyers bidding simultaneously on your property. If I succeed you will get the highest price the market can bear for your property.

"If you would like to list with my firm, I can go see your property next week and tell you whether I can take the listing. If I do list it, I will give you a summary of every showing and all feedback from the market in the form of a weekly verbal update and a monthly written update. Here is my card and my cell phone number."

"That's a bargain. Why don't you charge more?" he asked.

The question took me aback, and I was momentarily speechless.

"Do you have an agreement for me to sign?"

"Yes, here." I said and gave him our agreement.

I briefly informed him of the default clause and commissions due us and other obligations that we discussed in the previous chapter.

"Anything else?" he asked.

"No," I said.

"Here." He pushed the signed contract across the desk. *"This is the caretaker's number and my cell number. Call me after you have seen it and tell me what price I can get for it. I want it under contract in thirty days."*

I called him the following week and told him that the property would fetch about $1.7M on a thirty-day sale. I also told him that because he was going for a discounted quick sale price in thirty days, he did not necessarily need me, nor did he have to pay the premium commission we charged. He could list it locally at 6 percent and would probably get the price I suggested. I said that I could recommend to him a very good local agent.

"No, I want you to handle it," he said. *"Just call me when you get it done."*

Because I priced the property to sell within thirty days as instructed, we had three offers on the property within two weeks. I negotiated a sale in the third week and went to contract in the fourth at full price.

I never met my client again. He did, however, send me a note that said,

"Good job. You listened when I told you ninety seconds and thirty days. You should charge more next time. Regards, Mark."

While I will be the first to admit that this sale was every real estate agent's dream listing (and I've never had a similar experience since), it taught me this valuable lesson: wealthy, busy people want to hire others who are competent, succinct, and get them to their goal. They are happy to pay extra for that service and expertise.

Commissions will go up and down depending on the listing climate at the time and the listing agent, but given the risks of marketing a luxury property, consider charging a higher commission or at a minimum a non-discounted one.

Because so few agents articulate or even know the goal of all luxury *power marketing*—multiple buyers bidding simultaneously or the threat thereof—and do not know how to get to this point, clarifying that goal for sellers and providing them the focus for all marketing activities, in itself, justifies a generous commission. Even a standard commission on a three times average price home, while a non-standard amount, is justified by the extra value and dollars *power marketing* brings. Recall my wife Linda's story of getting almost 25 percent more for her client just by making a series of last calls and orchestrating the bids. Recall how making the last call for Clarendon Court added $250,000 of extra value. Was not the stepladder marketing that resulted in the sale of *Le Domaine Résistance* worth the extra commission? Implementing what you have learned here provides exemplary extra value not found in the average agent pool.

> Implementing what you have learned here provides exemplary extra value not found in the average agent pool.

I am certain that it was the last point that my seller above meant by his suggestion that I should charge more. He was collecting million-dollar commissions as an investment banker at Goldman. He knew that what I said was outside the usual agent-speak. He wanted that and knew that for him to spend time on this sale was not economically wise. For these benefits he was more than willing to pay.

If you, too, can provide such value, then a higher commission should be yours. You just have to make sure that a higher commission is as matter of fact in your listing presentation as the value you now can articulate.

By reading this book and implementing its best practices, you are going to join an elite group of marketing consultants. Getting a higher commission is about being paid for that rarified expertise you now provide.

12

Tips for the Rookie and the Pro

Despite the greater risks involved in working in luxury real estate, buyers, sellers, agents, and developers still want to be in this market for the glamour and prestige. As an agent, you are confronted with an additional reason: the simple financial fact that while a $3 million property takes longer to show, requires more money, and requires greater skill than, say, a $300,000 property, still, you get paid ten times more.

And you like that. So you decide to focus on the luxury market, yet you don't belong to the fancy clubs and don't hang around with movie stars or Wall Street moguls on a daily basis. How do you gain entry to this elite club? Let's begin with the most difficult situation, the agent who has little or no experience in the luxury real estate market. What should the rookie do?

Tip for the Rookie

An agent I know in Greenwich was just starting his luxury marketing career some twenty years ago. He read books, listened to tapes, went to seminars, and did everything else he could to prep himself for getting into luxury real estate. Then he met the top agent in his office.

"Hey, kid," she said. "When I follow you into that living room, who do you think they are going to list with? The guy in training or the person with the track record? I can answer that for you. It's going to be me."

Those encouraging words of warning from the top agent in his office may not be typical of top agents everywhere, but I can assure you that if the competition gets rough, accomplished agents always pull out the greater experience argument. They will also throw in the fact that they have more market share. Then they will top off their presentation with the "look at what I sold recently" argument. This all means that, yes, they will probably win against the rookie.

And that is the whole point. If they have the winning armaments in this battle, then get them on your side so you, too, can win. Don't fight the skilled, experienced agents; make them your allies by approaching them to share a listing. Yes, you will give up 25 percent or 33 percent or maybe even 50 percent of a listing. But with the other agent's experience, you will probably get the assignment. With your new *power marketing* skills, you will also sell it. And that is how you get into the upper end luxury market—a little like stepladder marketing, one rung at a time. There will come a time when you won't need help getting up the ladder, but until you have your own track record of success, the easiest way to get up the ladder is by asking for (and paying for) someone else's help.

> If they have the winning armaments in this battle, then get them on your side so you, too, can win. Don't fight the skilled, experienced agents; make them your allies by approaching them to share a listing.

The Rookie Asks a Question

When I was working the North Shore of Long Island, I was asked to be the guest breakfast speaker at a Long Island multi-office firm that had a very limited track record of luxury sales. At the end of my talk, I invited anyone with a potential listing to speak with me. One nicely dressed woman with a charming smile came up.

Somewhat apologetically she admitted that she had been in the business only six to eight months and had no experience in the higher end. She said that she had been at her son's private school the prior week and overheard another parent say that she and her husband might be interested in selling their home. While she had never been to the property, she had seen it through the gates and thought that it would probably qualify. She wanted to know what to say to the seller.

I told her to call the seller and introduce herself as the mother of a student attending the same school.

"Tell her that you could not help but overhear that she might be interested in selling her property." Then I instructed her to say the following:

"My firm is associated with a premier marketer of luxury real estate with one of the finest track records in the industry. Would it make sense for you to chat with them and see what they could do for you?"

The agent and I parted company; to be honest, I never thought I would hear anything more.

Several weeks later my phone rang. It was the agent calling to say that the seller was interested in meeting. When I called the seller to set up an appointment, I was told that the property was not on the market officially because they wanted an aggressive price and they did not need to sell. It was the typical luxury homeowner refrain. And so Bob Borden and I rode out to Old Brookville, Long Island, New York, following the agent's directions to Sunninghill Farm.

It is so ironic that Sunninghill Farm was brought to us by a rookie agent and also sold by a sole proprietor agent who, while not a rookie, was inexperienced in selling luxury real estate. (Recall the agent in Chapter 6 with the roadside shack for an office.)

That sale was not only a triumph for my firm, but for this wonderful rookie agent as well.

Leveraging Another's Track Record

Her story illustrates the simplest way for a rookie agent to enter the luxury field: do it with someone who has a track record. Leverage that track record and skill to get the job done, and use a successful sale to launch your career. Don't ignore this tactic because you dislike sharing the spotlight with others. As this story shows, almost anyone can pick up a lead, but not everyone can turn it into something.

To gain entry to the luxury market team up with an experienced professional either in your office or with your company's luxury marketing division.[30] Create a team for your first listing or your first few. You can take credit for the sales, and you will have a cornucopia of color brochures of million-dollar-and-up properties now to present as yours. Your sharing with others will not lessen how others view you, but instead, will demonstrate the inclusiveness of your listing approach.

What you lose in sharing your commission will be more than compensated by shortening your lead time in establishing your luxury marketing career. Most importantly, you will have a better chance at listing the property and chalking up a success. It is better to have 50 percent of something than 100 percent of nothing, and it is better to start off with a string of successes, even if they're shared

Interview Your Firm; Sell the Team

Interview the high-end people at your firm and see with whom you feel most comfortable. Using someone's prior success is something even experienced agents do. At LandVest, we routinely used the successes of our colleagues to demonstrate examples of the lessons of this book. I have already related the story of how we used Jim Retz's story about listing President and Mrs. Reagan's house in Pacific Palisades. We all shared John Coburn's sale of the $10.8M Gimble family estate in Greenwich and Wade Staniar's listing of portions of the Rockefeller family's Adirondack estate as examples of the kind of work our firm did. Similarly, we all delighted in mentioning that our president, Dick Perkins, had Jacqueline Onassis as a client. Every major sale and client of the firm was a sale or a client of the team. We made it a practice to sell our team, rather than just our individual successes.

If you are new to luxury marketing, the experience of others is gold. You should regularly document sales by others in your office and present them in your listing presentation folder. There is no harm in showing a seller that not only are you part of a team, but a very successful one at that.

> If you are new to luxury marketing, the experience of others is gold.

Sell a Track Record Beyond the Local Market

I should also mention that there is a real advantage to having non-local successes. Indeed, we often sold our "greater than local" knowledge. In new markets, such as the greater New York area for which I was responsible, we routinely built our reputation upon the sales of colleagues in other markets. We could do this because the players within these markets traveled in such close circles. Knowing what was going on in the Nantucket or Cape Cod luxury markets was both interesting and relevant to a seller in the Hamptons or on the North Shore because it gave reassurance to the seller that by listing with us she was gaining access to elite circles outside her local market.

The same is true anywhere. Providing greater than local knowledge helps to put your local knowledge in perspective and serves as a point of differentiation from the competition.

Doing It Without a Track Record

Now assume that neither you, nor anyone in your firm or office, has any track record off of which to piggyback. As a result, you cannot bring in someone with whom to share the listing. Let me use the example I faced while building our greater New York operations as we routinely moved into new markets. Sellers said to me daily,

"I don't know you and you have no track record of selling in this market. Why should I list with you?"

Indeed, I heard this objection over and over for six years in every new market we entered. When you don't have existing market share, clients tend to believe their market is so different that no matter how successful the marketing techniques, they don't believe those techniques will work in their market.

The simple answer to this objection is to do some listening and reflect back the argument as made. For example:

"Let me understand your point. Because we have not worked in this market before, you don't think these marketing techniques will work here and you don't want to be the first to try. Right?"

"I can appreciate your concerns and fears. I, too, would feel the same way if I were in your position, so let me ask you this: Who do you think will work harder to get your property sold, someone already in the area or someone who wants to establish a track record here? Is it someone who already has plenty of local references or someone who wants you as a reference to build their business?

By acknowledging an objection, people stop thinking about it and instead turn their attention to your response.

"I am looking for two things. First, I want to gain your trust and sell your property. Second, by selling your property, I want to establish my track record in this market. I want ten more properties in the next twelve months.

"I can only do this if someone first gives me a chance to apply proven marketing techniques that work in every market, all the time. In return for giving me that chance, you will be the recipient of more services, exposure, and attention than anyone because I cannot fail to sell your property. I am building a business and reputation in this market, and your listing is vital to creating my track record."

The above argument is tempting. The consumer can get more value for the same commission. This argument sells value to highly sophisticated and smart people, just as in the example of the buyers of Clarendon Court and *Le Domaine Résistance.*

Businesspeople Understand Business Building

High-end consumers understand your desire to build a business because many of them did just that. By providing the clients with this rationale, you allow them to evaluate your motivation just as you are evaluating theirs. They will appreciate your commitment to success.

They also know that you want them as references. That gives them a feeling of control over your future—not an unimportant sense of power when dealing with the major egos you often encounter in luxury real estate.

In this regard, breaking into the luxury market is no different from breaking into other industries: demonstrate a motivation that is compelling, provide good value for the money spent, sell the property, and then get written references and testimonials to show to the next client.

Market Knowledge

Another convincing way any rookie can enter the luxury market is through sheer market knowledge. You can "wow" someone with your knowledge of the market without necessarily having listed or sold anything. This kind of expertise can be demonstrated using statistics, graphs, charts, and pictures. These can include the following:

- How many sales occurred last year over $1M? Over $2M? Over $3M? Over $4M, etc. in your market?

- Keep a list of those sales.

- Call the agents to ask where the buyers came from.

- Calculate how much income it takes for someone to afford a $1M home? $2M? $3M, etc.

- The days on market for luxury listings.

- Keep track of the percentage of asking price sellers receive. This is called the "list to sell ratio."

Doing Market Research First

When I first entered the market on Long Island's North Shore, I researched every sale over $1M. Initially I did this to see how large the million-dollar market was. This research gave me not just a wealth of information, but it was also highly valuable to sellers and buyers.

> You can "wow" someone with your knowledge of the market without necessarily having listed or sold anything.

To my surprise, we were one of only two firms (the other was an appraisal firm) compiling and continually updating this data. Most luxury agents didn't bother to gather data and assess it objectively. In at least this one way, it was easier for us (the experts from afar) to be more impartial.

From this research I knew the average number of luxury properties sold yearly. I learned about the many submarkets that exist within one region or geographic market—for instance, that while there was an active market in Kings Point, brokerage commissions had become so cutthroat, and in some cases were discounted so low, that it was a poor choice for us to invest much time or money.

I discovered that the million-dollar market effectively stopped at Huntington, Long Island, and that listing anything farther east over $1M was risky. I studied the relationship between waterfront and inland estate properties to see what ratios applied and looked closely at underlying land values since land appreciates over time, but not the improvements (which often depreciate with obsolescence).

Once I had established values for waterfront and inland parcels, it was relatively easy to add on the improvement values and determine the core book values and valuation ranges. Once I understood the core valuation ranges, it was only a matter of interviewing the clients to determine their motivation before recommending the appropriate listing price within those ranges. Research also included calculating average appreciation and depreciation rates, and noting which sub-markets had the highest rates of appreciation. This told me where I could price properties more aggressively and where to be less aggressive. If I priced a property aggressively in an appreciating market, the rising market would often bail me out of any pricing mistakes.

I also looked at how much buildable land was still left and what the pipeline of building lots was at the local planning board to see if there would be much new supply coming on. I researched consumer preferences (by calling and interviewing other agents) to determine if there was some type of property that the market particularly liked but which was not readily available. In this way I learned what could cause a stir if it came to market and might sell relatively quickly.

To return to the Sunninghill Farm example, when we saw the twenty-eight acres in a two-acre zone, we immediately knew what to advise our seller: that the property not only had a subdivision value, but that it had a scarcity value that exceeded its development potential. That scarcity value came from the small number of estates on the North Shore boasting the kind of acreage Sunninghill Farm offered. There were many powerful and wealthy people who wanted the privacy and panache of a great estate and would pay up for it by either recombining already subdivided property or paying a scarcity premium for an unsubdivided, intact, large landed estate. We never would have known this without doing prior research and would not have been able to advise our seller prudently.

Additional Benefits of Being an Expert

Researching and quantifying local and regional market data provides numerous additional benefits.

First, comparatively speaking, you rise above other agents who, for lack of such data, are less able to take as objective a look at their market.

Second, a review of every sale over the last two years with drive-by inspections gives you a plethora of visual references about which you can speak authoritatively.

Third, the data enables you to answer questions from sellers about "that property that sold last year." It allows you to confirm information or correct rumors with facts. This is especially true when the seller thinks a property sold for more than it actually did and wants to price a house based upon this erroneous information.

Most importantly for a rookie, this knowledge can overcome a less than robust sales record, as sellers are less likely to question the track record of someone perceived as a market expert.

Knowledge is not only worthy unto itself, it is also power. Accurate market data, presented visually to sellers in pie charts and graphs, can provide the authority needed to gain entry into the luxury real estate market. Remember, initially I had no sales on the North Shore of Long Island, just data. You, too, can create a fantastic monthly or quarterly report of market data for upscale homeowners.[31] I assure you they will be fascinated by it.

In addition, create a data base of homeowners comprising your luxury market (using whichever definition you find appropriate). The data can be compiled from either MLS information or by spending time at Town Hall, the assessor's office, or the county registry of deeds. With computer technology, this is an easy task. Working full time, I doubt it will take more than five to ten working days to gather the information and create a solid database of high-end homeowners that will be your "farm" area. Another week should be spent locating the sold properties and doing the drive-bys.

This information will serve you well with upscale buyers, especially if you also act as a buyer broker or employ one on your team. If you have no listings yet to promote, then at least you can promote your knowledge of the market as a service to buyers. That service will be as good an advertisement as any and can distinguish you in any buyer's mind as not just another agent. Instead, you are offering a service that is essential to buyers—interpreting data to help them make wise decisions.

Such buyers will someday become luxury homeowners who can act as references for you, and possibly, as sellers themselves. Once you start securing listings, you can switch hats and hand your buyer brokerage business over to another agent who works for your team, while you continue focusing on listing luxury properties and selling your *power marketing* skills.

Personal Marketing Your Market Knowledge

Providing good, timely information should be the foundation of your personal marketing strategy. Every three months, issue an update on the luxury market for the benefit of your local papers, and even non-local media.

For example, when trying to establish ourselves in the Hamptons on eastern Long Island, one year we issued a press release on the top ten listings currently available in the marketplace. We simply listed the ten properties, their price, a picture, and the listing broker. We had only two of the top ten listings, but the story was so interesting that *Newsday* picked it up, and while they interviewed other brokers in addition to us, they published pictures of our two properties and gave us top billing. Because the story allowed us to be perceived as the market experts, our phone began to ring steadily. Remember, the listings do not have to be yours to indicate what is available and to comment on it. It is all public information.

You can do the same with the top ten sales in your market every year. My former colleague Jim Retz used to keep a list of the top ten sales nationally; once a year he issued the list in a press release that made for fascinating reading. It did not matter if they were his sales or not; he compiled and provided the information and was, therefore, the expert.

You should also take an expansive view of the possibilities that stem from your data. You need not confine yourself to the print media. Every local television reporter should have your contact information for interviews and sound bites, especially if you are in a high-profile luxury market.

One of my former Greenwich sales agents, Bill Andruss, regularly appeared on a local radio talk show about the real estate market and particularly the high end. Now he has taken over the show. Why not suggest to your local radio station that you host a weekly talk show where viewers can call in and ask questions about the market? You also can invite appraisers, home inspectors, lawyers, or decorators to be your guests and talk about luxury real estate. Or maybe your local newspaper or lifestyle magazine wants a regular contributor to write a real estate column. Offering solid advice is not only good publicity, but it is also the foundation for future leads.

Opportunities abound for exposure associated with market expertise and closed sales. Being a market expert is ideal personal marketing because it is without hype and without boasting. You become the knowledgeable provider of luxury home information—the best reputation to have.

The Power of Stance

I began this chapter with the rookie, the person without any experience at the luxury end of the market. But after you develop market expertise, the jitters of your "rookie-ness" will melt away. By being the compiler, curator, and interpreter of vital market information, you will develop a new stance. You will be the consultative expert who can and should command a premium commission for a premium service. When you enter that seller's living room, your body language will say that you are bringing something to the table that is much needed. Having this stance is critical for gaining sellers' confidence.

By being the compiler, curator, and interpreter of vital market information, you will develop a new stance. You will be the consultative expert who can and should command a premium commission for a premium service.

Market knowledge also provides the best foundation for pricing. With it you are able to deliver prudent advice to buyers and sellers. You avoid getting into the wild speculations about pricing luxury real estate that often characterize the industry, grounding you in the hard facts of reality. The whole brokerage industry cannot help but be bettered in the process.

> Armed with luxury market data you are the market expert, which, when combined with *power marketing* techniques and then married to your networking and social skills, provides everything for *power marketing* success.

Tip for the Pro

For all you experienced agents who look at those newbies gnawing at your backside trying to get into your market, here is my advice. Don't try to kick them off the ladder. Don't try to keep them down. Instead, welcome them. Reach out to them. Encourage them to invite you to be their partner when they get leads.

> Encourage them to invite you to be their partner when they get leads.

After all, those newbies represent the future. They have the drive and the energy that you may now start to lack. But you have the skill, the track record, the market share that speaks to sellers. So combine their energy with your track record, and you will gain even more market share, make even more money, and quite possibly line up someone to whom you can sell your book of business contacts someday.

Some Agents Do It Differently: How One Successful Listing and Selling Agent Works

Years ago I attended the funeral of a member of one of America's first families. The reception was held at an exclusive club, and present were a Who's Who of the social and financial elite of the East Coast. Also present was one of the most successful luxury agents of all time, someone whom I had watched from a distance and whose success was unquestionable and enviable.

This agent thrived at listing so many multi-million-dollar properties that her annual income was reportedly between $1 million and $3 million. However, in the minds of the agent community, she achieved this success by habitually overpricing properties or selling ones before anyone else knew they might be coming to market. While both actions annoyed local agents, selling properties that never hit the market was particularly infuriating. I had always wanted to know how she did it; the reception afforded the perfect opportunity.

For two hours I tactfully followed her around the room, discreetly eavesdropping to overhear what so many luxury homeowners found so convincing.

Creating "Urgency" to Act

Here was a master networker. What I learned was that she embraced a core *power marketing* principal, the need to create urgency to act. Indeed, she created it through a kind of teasing of clients into wanting to sell or buy by putting them to the blush. She rattled them by bringing something to their attention that, in turn, created a motivation to buy and to sell.

The dialogue went something like this:[32] *"Renee, so good to see you again. How are the children? The dog? That problem with the pool you were trying to solve...?"* The usual small talk. Then she would say, *"You know I was thinking about you and Mike and that beautiful home of yours..."* engaging the seller in a conversation about how she loved their house.

She then turned the conversation. *"I was thinking the other day about when you bought that property. So many years ago! Now, your husband is a managing director and you are such a stellar host and philanthropist. Perhaps it's time to consider a move. Maybe to a house that speaks more to your current situation...?"*

But then, she delivered the coup de grace. *"I just happened to be in a home the other day that made me think of you both. I was standing in this gorgeous dining room, and I imagined you holding the most magnificent dinner parties and receptions. And I thought to myself, this is where you should be now that you have the means to upgrade."*

I observed Renee's expression. You could see her thoughts whirl—how she and her husband were not living up to their proper social level and how much they needed to have their housing reflect their new social and financial status.

Status as a Motivator

Suddenly, you could see in her countenance the love for her home turning to concern. How could she possibly have tolerated their present conditions for so long, given their enhanced and rising circumstances? You could see the doubts bubble up about whether guests had been coming to their home and left wondering if the dining room was really too small or the views not adequate. As doubts grew to fears, one could imagine the dinner conversation that night.

In this way a master networker and influencer was tilting someone's thoughts toward moving. Suddenly, two people who had never thought of selling their home were possible buyers. They were thinking about going out to see a better property, which up to that moment they had been too blind to realize they needed. The agent had enlightened them to the need for a bigger and better place to live.

As a result of conversations like these, homeowners who never thought about buying again were out looking at properties with her. This agent also knew that if she could sell them a different home, there was the sale of their current one, which only she knew might be available.

Just as *power marketers* focus on creating an urgency to act through competition, this master was creating an urgency to buy and then an urgency to sell based upon "move-up status," instead of competition. She was overcoming the lack of urgency to buy and the lack of urgency to sell in one social engagement. The result of her efforts was two to five sales every year that were unlisted.

Few agents have the capability to maneuver like this, and I certainly don't approve of any property not being exposed to the whole market. But she did understand that luxury buyers and sellers in her very small market lack urgency to act. By understanding this difference, this master networker came up with a different way to overcome it.

Create a Written Marketing Plan

Over the years I have found that upscale clients and their advisers (legal and financial) expect a written marketing plan, often attached to the listing agreement. I have always had handy a generic one that can be customized for each seller. It is available at *http://PowerMarketing.pro.* I urge you to have one always ready.

Written plans memorialize your intended activities and allow you to remind sellers of the need for a different approach. They allow you to restate in writing the goal of all marketing activities (by now, you know what that is). They also allow you to reflect things said by the sellers in interviews, (e.g., that they want to be out in ninety days or that they believe their property has such and such advantages over others).[33]

Personally, I am not afraid of length. To put a weighty proposal in front of someone who is contemplating selling their $5M to $10M luxury home seems like a reasonable thing to do. Though it may not be read in full, weight and volume can demonstrate your seriousness.

Presenting the Marketing Plan

Some agents and firms adorn their marketing plans with something that instantly gets others' attention and helps to differentiate them in the marketplace. One example is the Tiffany-style box that Coldwell Banker Previews devised for presenting their luxury marketing plans.

The marketing plan came in a high-quality royal blue box tied with white ribbon that arrived prior to the listing appointment like a special gift. When the seller unwrapped the box and folded back the tissue paper, it revealed a beautifully designed Previews marketing piece done in water-color with illustrations of luxury properties. It was on thick parchment-like paper; the touch and feel were instantly upscale. It was quite a showstopper.

Today, for a small sum you can order off the Internet other types of presentations, such as a bound book with your marketing plan and extensive photos of the property. This presentation can also serve as a memento for the seller. These sorts of marketing ploys do help distinguish you from other agents. But market knowledge and an understanding of *power marketing* provide the most convincing tools to truly stand apart.

On Chattiness

Few things differentiate the pro from the rookie more distinctly than chattiness. Real estate agents are like most people. We talk too much and ask too few questions. Chattiness may be interpreted as a sign of weakness (especially by foreigners), whereas saying less (or even nothing) is often a sign of strength. Chattiness can more often reveal how little we know, rather than how much. A good rule is to make sure that we have left others their turns to speak. As is often said, we have two ears and one mouth, and we should use them in that proportion.

On Relations with Other Agents

Never offend or betray the brokerage community. In your good relations with them lies some of the marketing power you bring to your clients. As a seller, whenever I interview an agent to list my own property, I am keenly interested in how he is perceived by his peers. A poorly respected agent is never going to be able to enlist the brokerage community's support for my property, an important aspect to a successful sale.

   You should be conscious of the fact that you are not likely to produce the buyer. Rather, it is other agents who have the buyer. You must cultivate a reputation for integrity with your peers by returning phone calls, being as candid as you can without violating your fiduciary responsibilities, and always acting with kindness and fairness. In the end a powerful reason for any seller to hire you is for your good relations with those who might have the buyer.

On What You Say About Others

Some competitors try to build their reputations by abusing others. The Code of Ethics of the National Association of Realtors is clear on how to act toward others. Article 15 states, "Realtors shall not knowingly or recklessly make false or misleading statements about competitors, their business, or their business practices."[34] In addition, the code asserts that it is your duty not to discredit or bring dishonor to the real estate profession as a whole and not to make unsolicited comments about other practitioners. When asked by clients about others, it is your duty only to provide opinions that are objective, professional in manner, and uninfluenced by personal motivation or potential advantage.

While badmouthing competitors will be found in all businesses and walks of life, it is always better to focus on the value of what you propose than on the weaknesses and faults of others. Smart and sophisticated clientele are more enlightened by your expertise and the wisdom of your insights than by comments about others.

Tips on the Listing Presentation

I began this book by differentiating *power marketing* from property marketing and personal marketing. While the best property marketing comes from those who engage in the *power marketing* techniques found here, similarly the best personal marketing comes from having a reputation for being a *power marketer.* But you can't employ property, personal, or *power marketing* without getting through the listing appointment. Here is a tip for that event.

On Eagerness to List

Whenever you get a lead on a million-dollar-or-more home, it is hard not to drop everything, including common sense, and rush to list the property. This is a mistake. It is better to thank the potential client for thinking of you first. Then say that you want to see the property and meet with her to determine if you can be of help. *"Let me come out to see the property and meet with you, and then I can tell you if my services will align with your goals."*

You really do not know if you can be of assistance to her, nor whether you are the right match for her needs and goals. You first have to assess the property and her motivations. So begin by admitting it and plan on asking the necessary questions to determine if this is right for both of you.

Over-eagerness to get a listing often forces the agent to pay a price in the terms of the listing agreement, the length of time, marketing expenses to be incurred, and the heightened expectations of the seller. This creates a high cost for the listing and can limit the likelihood of success. Francis Bacon says, "Fortune is like the market, where many times, if you can stay a little, the price will fall."[35] So, too, if agents are more circumspect, the financial, emotional, and reputational "cost" of the listing might fall and increase the likelihood of success.

Questions and More Questions, Only Rarely Answers

Listing appointments should begin with questions and rely on them as the primary form of communication throughout. When I had ninety seconds with the Goldman Sachs investment banker, this was hardly possible, but most of the time agents have more than a minute and half. Start with questions, as Bob Borden did for Clarendon Court.

> Listing appointments should begin with questions and rely on them as the primary form of communication throughout.

Someone who begins with questions creates a process in which others are encouraged to participate. By answering your questions, others also get to listen to someone they prefer to hear anyway—themselves. The more they do so, the more knowledge you gain of the situation, their motivation, and the likelihood of a sale. The bulk of my course in book form "*Winning Listing Presentations*" consists of scripts made up of such questions. It is available at http://PowerMarketing.pro.

On Doing Business with Friends

Real estate is said to be a business of relationships. As an agent you may be inclined to tell others how much you are loved by your clients and customers. While this is a powerful basis for some business, if you have friends just in order to have business, you will have them only until the real motive is detected.[36] I suggest that a quicker start for your seedling career is being a *power marketer*—someone with solid market data and marketing expertise. It can even compensate for not being in the clubs, the correct social circles or the gated communities.

Integrity Through Silence

Because you now own the *power marketing* keys to unlock the gates to luxury real estate marketing success, never reveal confidences about the private lives of those living beyond the gates. Your integrity as a luxury real estate *power marketer* depends on this. These are honored employments, always requiring discretion and often silence.

I have acknowledged the contributions and wisdom about marketing and sales that Wade Staniar, through his caring and mentoring over twenty-five years ago, provided me at the start of my career. It was also Wade who first taught me the phrases *"You cannot do good business with bad people"* and *"There is no commission worth your integrity."* Years of business dealings with thousands of clients have taught me the unfailing wisdom of those words, too.

The Takeaway _____

- Rookies should leverage another, more experienced agent's track record and bring in partners for the first few listings.

- Sell your firm's successes with you as part of a team.

- Provide not only local market knowledge but greater than local market knowledge for prospecting and differentiation.

- High-quality marketing plans, and company or personal marketing pieces can help to differentiate you.

- Don't be too eager to list before you even see the property or meet the seller. First determine whether you can be helpful in getting her closer to her goal.

- Pros should reach out and partner with rookies to help them ascend the ladder to luxury marketing success.

- Ask questions and listen.

- Never violate the confidences to which you will be privy.

- No commission is worth your integrity and you cannot do good business with bad people.

13

Postscript: Thoughts on Our Human Nature and Luxury Real Estate

I f there is any final lesson to be covered, it is that the luxury market provides an unusually fine stage for observing and understanding our all too personal longings, fears, hopes, and vainglory. Because wisdom about our basic human psyche is required in marketing, it doesn't hurt for a good agent to explore and understand a little about the basic insights and instincts behind our wanting luxury real estate.

The *Wealth* study indicated that there are powerful forces at work in luxury real estate that continually propel the rich to buck the advice of their financial counselors and over-invest in it. What are some of the underlying triggers and motivations of the rich that encourage them to love our product and cause them to defy their investment advisors? Let's try (ever so briefly) to understand the rich so we can better *power market* to them.

Marketing and Management

Marketing is the art of persuasion. When Marc Antony exclaimed, "Friends, Romans, countrymen. Lend me your ears," he was engaging in marketing. When Winston Churchill addressed his countrymen in World War II with such phrases as, "In War: Resolution. In Defeat: Defiance. In Victory: Magnanimity. In Peace: Good Will," he was marketing confidence and bedrock political values. When Franklin D. Roosevelt said, "The only thing we have to fear is fear itself," he was marketing hope.

> Wealthy people are not really so different from you or me; they are just other human beings that we are trying to persuade to do something.

Marketing is one of the most powerful tools of management. As indicated above, leaders engage in marketing as part of their management of the country. Usually they do what Roosevelt did and market hope. Demagogues usually market fear. Both are engaged in marketing as a primary means of managing people and actions. To market something is to understand the underlying human psychology—the fears and the benefits—of a potential action, and influence others to do our will.

As real estate agents we try to get sellers to list with us, brokers to cooperate with us to sell our properties, buyers to buy through us. In marketing to them, we are trying to manage them, to persuade them to do our bidding. Wealthy people are not really so different from you or me; they are just other human beings that we are trying to persuade to do something.

Some Causes for What We Do and How We Feel

Insight about ourselves comes from experience but especially from books written by great writers who have studied such things for a lifetime. I have many favorites, two of whom are Thomas Hobbes and Francis Bacon; and a third, Leo Strauss, relentlessly studied those two.

Hobbes was a great seventeenth-century English philosopher whose most famous work, *Leviathan,* was a study of human nature in two parts and a discussion of organizing politics based upon that nature. Francis Bacon was both a political man (Lord High Chancellor of Britain) and a great student of human nature. He wrote volumes of texts, but one book, *Essays or Counsels, Civil and Moral,* wittily dealt with a view of human nature similar to that of Hobbes and offered practical advice regarding it.

> To market something is to understand underlying human psychology.

Basic Instincts: What We Want and Need

According to Hobbes, acquisition, power, and lust for more are a foundational aspect of human nature. He observed that humans possess "a perpetual and restless desire of power after power, that ceaseth only in Death." Not only do we desire power (usually over others), but we "cannot assure the power and the means to live well...without the acquisition of more."[37]

Mankind's natural appetite for power through acquisitions, wrote Leo Strauss, has, as its basis, vanity, the love of one's own, especially oneself.[38]

In addition to this love of one's own and our desire for power, yet another expression of our humanity is the desire for honor. Honor is one way of gaining and demonstrating power and domination over others (precedence) and having it recognized by others.[39]

For our purposes, we would do well in understanding the field of luxury *power marketing* by starting with these primal insights: our lustful desire for power through acquisitions, our desire for precedence and domination through honor, and our love of ourselves—our vanity.

Distinguishing Oneself Through Luxury Real Estate

An avenue to indulge our passions and desires and gain this precedence over others comes from owning a piece of luxury real estate. Not only does it help to assuage somewhat these passions and desires, but doing so is relatively easy, requiring only money. No exceptional upbringing, no accident of birth, no special education is needed to buy (luxury) property. All you need is a bank account. With this simple acquisition, buyers can set themselves apart, indulge their pride and vanity, and acquire precedence and domination over others. With it one can wield social power and lord magnificence over many, not just those living in the immediate vicinity.

Our Democracy and Luxury Real Estate

A liberal democracy like ours has certain aspects that accentuate this primal importance of luxury real estate for satisfying these basic human desires. The modern democratic state has as its *raison d'etre* to keep in check our natural appetites, our pride, our vanity,[40] the very things that luxury real estate helps to express.

A liberal democratic state that looks upon all of us as equal when, in fact, our inner beings naturally long to differentiate and distinguish ourselves from others, creates an even greater need to set oneself apart in an attempt to be more unequal. For as Hobbes says, "If all things were equal in all men, nothing would be prized."[41]

Redirecting the Natural Appetites

Even though our natural appetites for power, precedence, love of ourselves, and honor are checked by the civil state, they still exist in us and have not been eliminated or destroyed.[42] The modern state recognizes this and tries to redirect them from antisocial, non-peaceful activities to peaceful ones in which they are vented and displayed—commercial or business activities, for example.

Indeed, the already-wealthy often consume themselves in the pursuit of business as the socially acceptable means to encourage and vent the indulgence of pride and vanity and engage the appetites for more. But even when our business is successful, we sometimes never fully satisfy the love of our own, our vanity, and the need for precedence over others around us. It is as if business—for all its power, prestige, and privilege—still doesn't sate human desires.

So, how do we fill that hole?

Acquiring, owning and displaying luxury real estate can be a peaceful and safe way for even the most ambitious to express power and domination in a liberal democracy. Pursuing luxury real estate can be one of the palliatives for innate desires. We should actually be grateful for this, because if the rich weren't preoccupied with their real estate, the passions for power, domination, distinguishing oneself from others, could be directed to other endeavors that might lead to great mischief and unsettling of a peaceful society.

Legitimizing Wealth

Luxury real estate also has a legitimizing role for wealth in every society. The wealthy, especially the newly wealthy, are interested in establishing equality with certain groups. For instance, by purchasing luxury real estate, the rich also legitimize their wealth among their peers and in their own eyes. Newer money wants to establish equality to others of equal standing or with old wealth. Owning a piece of luxury real estate can also help to legitimize the sometime circuitous route to the place achieved. "All rising to great place [is] by a winding stair," said Bacon.[43] The purchase of a piece of luxury real estate can be a palliative and a cure, mitigating the remembrance of such thoughts. Because it is also true that in the process of rising "by indignities men come to dignities,"[44] it can provide a kind of veil over an ascent that is not always so glamorous.

Selling to Keep Something

But having riches can also mean that we can become gripped by the anxiety of keeping them (or worse, losing them). For instance, it is natural for anyone with riches to fall into spending them, which can also lead to spending more than we have. It is intemperance that characterizes most wealth, and it does not stop with the getting, but continues regardless of how much we have gotten. As Bacon reminds us, "Prosperity doth best discover vice."[45]

Inheriting Anxiety

Even inherited wealth has its share of anxiety. Those who inherit often wonder why the accident of birth shined on them and why they received wealth for which they have not expended any efforts, except to be born and to live. Uncertainty and vulnerability thus often comes with inheritance.

Competition and Unleashing It

The most central principle for *power marketing* is competition. While our anxieties are often as great as our desires, competition involves both desire and anxiety. For as Hobbes says, "...if any two men desire the same thing, which nevertheless they cannot both enjoy [they] endeavor to destroy or subdue one another."[46] This is a reminder of how intense and powerful the competition for the same object can become! Wanting the same thing releases ferocity of spirit that can quickly overcome any notions of value and reasonableness.

At the upper end of the market, where having the means (weapons) is not a problem, the competition can become more fierce. Here, the desire to win can be stronger than the ability to act rationally. *Power marketing* comes from our ability to organize matters in the real estate transaction so that we can release this intense competition and prevent any actions that mitigate it.

The desire to win a competition can become totally encompassing and take on a life all its own. Power can become more than a means and become the end in itself. A competitive situation, i.e., a *power marketing* situation, unleashes a whole series of emotional, intellectual and passionate strategies simply to win. At such times, our brains become but the maidservants to our desires.

This whole book has demonstrated the importance of understanding competition as the core of our *power marketing* success.

Having an Audience for Comparison

It is impossible to understand luxury real estate without understanding our human need for an audience. Our power and desire to dominate or gain precedence over others has the corollary that we need others to recognize that precedence. Those marvelous gates to a great estate may have been created not so much to keep others out as to provide a billboard for power, on display for the audience that drives by. Hobbes went so far as to even say that man's joy "consists in comparing himself with other men...."[47] To do so, we need other men present; we value at least their forming an audience and hope for their applause. We value their validation, their approval, even if privately we are inclined to believe we do not need it.

Establishing Ourselves Apart and Above

The luxury home, the grand estate, has been a way to classify ourselves apart from others for millennia. It is a way to establish our superiority, our inequality, our precedence over others around us. The need to engage in these kinds of comparisons is at the core of human nature. It is the ever-present desire for power, precedence, and domination over others by the attainment of glory, honor, and dignity through which we seek to satisfy love of ourselves, inclining humanity toward the world of luxury real estate. Consequently, the luxury home becomes much more than just our castle.

For the most ambitious and talented, a luxurious home is a trophy of differentiation and distinction. It also offers the hope of some protection from the affairs that allowed the rich to buy it and the business perils that always seem to lie in wait, possibly to take it away. In our modern democratic world, it is as public a display as was a chest full of medals in an aristocratic or monarchic day. It is simultaneously a repose to shut out the world and find one's peace, offering the security which rising to great place and great riches may not. Here is where we can rest from the climb, and where others can still view us with awe.

Comments?
Go to www.PowerMarketing.pro/Comments and
tell me what you think.

Appendix

Using "Average" versus "Median" Price for a Definition of Luxury Real Estate

Allow me to explain why I prefer to use a definition for luxury real estate of "two to three times the average price" instead of using "two to three times the median price." As we all know "median" is the price point where 50 percent of the properties trade above and 50 percent below that price. "Average price" is calculated by taking all the sales in any market, totaling their value, and then dividing that summary value by the number of sales to arrive at an average. Both are reported by the National Association of Realtors® and most local Multiple Listing Services.

If we use "two to three times median price" as our base criteria, several things happen. First, we end up statistically not very far from the same place as the "top 10 percent definition." That gets us right back to having millions of homes counted as "luxury" that are not, the total of which far exceeds even the most generous calculation by the Federal Reserve and the Census. It thus drops our price point and trivializes the exclusive nature of luxury real estate.

Some agents like to use median rather than average price because it is not affected much, if at all, by the occasional periods when a few sales at the extreme end of the market allegedly "skew" the average price. As the argument goes, the average price can be too affected by such sales; therefore, it does not give an accurate reading on the market, whereas the median price gives such sales little consequence and is only mini-mally affected.

The fact that average price is affected by such occasional large sales (and median is not) is the very reason that I *prefer* to use it.

True, if we have a $40M sale in Greenwich, it absolutely "skews" the average price by pushing it up. I would argue, however, that by "skewing" the average price upward, such sales raise the bar—thereby making it more challenging for properties to fall into the "luxury" category under my "two to three times average price" definition. We want those big sales factored into our definition of the luxury market because they often set a new standard for a market; they often reflect new plateaus that buyers are willing to pay. We want our definition to be sensitive to such raised bars and new plateaus—and only the average price accommodates that. I would argue even further that such sales also raise the expectation of what a luxury property is in any market.

If we are confronted with those circumstances where such a skew-ing by one or two sales of the average price truly distorts the representa-tion of even the high end of the market, possibly because there might be so few luxury sales at one time in one market area, this significant discrepancy usually lasts only for one or two quarters—or at most four. We should be able to adjust our presentations to our sellers when this occurs and explain what the skewed data represents, e.g., a once in a lifetime $40M sale in a market where the average might be only $$1.3M. In addition, we can always smooth out such averages and look at them in the context of six months or one year.

Thus, I feel luxury is best reflected in average price and can be mar-ginalized by using the median price. By using average price, we keep the definition of what constitutes luxury luxurious.

Let's assume that we create an index[48] that utilizes a multiple of two and a half times *average price* and apply it to some different markets.

Lancaster, Pennsylvania If the average price for all property in Lancaster, Pennsylvania, is $270,000, then a property would qualify for being in the luxury real estate market if it were likely to sell for $675,000 or more. If there are none, so be it.

Manhattan, New York In 2008 the average price was $1,590,000; therefore, any property over $4M would initially qualify. By 2010 it had dropped to $1,350,000; therefore any property over $3.3M would qualify.

Greenwich, Connecticut In 2010 the average home price was $2.5M; as a result the luxury end is over $6.250,000.

Beverly Hills, California In 2010 the average price was $3,066,734, making luxury real estate initially defined as over $7.5M.

Hollywood, California In 2010 Hollywood enjoyed an average price of $1,030,000, making luxury real estate anything over $2.5M.

Palm Beach, Florida In 2009 the average single family home sold for $3.4M; as a result the luxury market would be constituted by those sales over $8.5M.

Dallas, Texas In 2010 the average sales price was about $420,000; therefore at two and a half times average price the luxury market would be those homes over $1M.

Endnotes & Citations

1. Thomas Hobbes, Leviathan Parts I and II (New York: Bobbs-Merrill, 1958), p. 68.
2. Francis Bacon, *Essays,* see "Of Expense," (New York: The Odyssey Press, 1937), p. 32. Bacon says, "Riches are for spending..."
3. Zhu Xiao Di, "Million Dollar Homes and Wealth in the United States," Joint Center on Housing Studies, Harvard University, January 2004.
4. U.S. Bureau of the Census, *U.S. Census of Population and Housing 2000* (Washington, DC: Government Printing Office, 2000).
5. Zhu Xiao Di, "Million Dollar Homes and Wealth in the United States," p. 2.
6. Brian K. Bucks, Arthur B. Kennickell, Traci L. Mach ,and Kevin B. Moore, "Changes in U.S. Family Finances from 2004 to 2007: Evidence from the Survey of Consumer Finances," *Federal Reserve Bulletin,* 95 (February 2009), A1–A55.
7. Zhu Xiao Di, "Million Dollar Homes and Wealth in the United States," p. 2.
8. This figure includes condominiums and multi-family, whereas the U.S. Census data only uses "single-family owner-occupied" to define the overall market.
9. Associates of Merrill Lynch and Capgemini, *Wealth: How the World's High-Net-Worth Grow, Sustain and Manage their Fortunes,* (Mississauga, Ontario, Canada: John Wiley & Sons, 2008).
10. "State of the World's Wealth," *Wealth Report 2009* (Merrill Lynch Global Wealth Management and Capgemini, 2009), pp. 2–6. The report updated figures as of 2008. In 2008 the 10 million HNWIs

shrunk by 14.9 percent to 8.6 million, and their wealth dropped to $32.8 trillion. For the purposes of this book, the trend is the same and the fluctuations are not central. *Wealth* forecasts that by 2012, HNWIs' financial wealth will recover to $48.5 trillion, see p. 5.

11. Thomas J. Stanley and William D. Danko, *The Millionaire Next Door* (New York: Pocket Books, 1996).

12. I am compiling evidence from the field and will update my website with new findings at http://PowerMarketing.pro.

13. Kirk Henckels, "Luxury Residential Report, Overview of the 2008 Luxury Market" January 1, 2009, Accessed August 13, 2009 at www.stribling.com, p. 1.

14. Josh Barbanel, "At Long Last, a Leveling Out?" *New York Times*, September 27, 2009.

15. See Chapter 13, "Postscript."

16. Some years ago I was pleased to see Prudential Real Estate actually embrace band pricing. There are problems with doing so—specifically that buyers like to have a target listing price. Nonetheless, band pricing should still be part of every CMA and BPO.

17. For a list of seller motivations, see http://PowerMarketing.pro.

18. The "driver" wants to know "How?" and is bottom-line oriented. The "expressive" wants to know "What if?" and likes turning ideas into action. The "amiable" asks "Why?' and wants things done harmoniously and be personally involved. The "analytical" asks "What?" and wants to excel at creating models and thinking through concepts.

19. See *Global Connections: Marketing Homes Internationally* at http://PowerMarketing.pro, due early 2012.

20. Throughout this book I have utilized the technique of writer's license to reconstruct dialogue as faithfully as my memory serves.

21. Dominick Dunne, "Sunny Memories," *Vanity Fair* online, January 30, 2009.

22. Note 20 applies to all dialogue throughout this chapter.

23. To purchase a document that your attorney can customize to state licensing laws and the MLS rules, go to http://PowerMarketing.pro.

24. *Economist's Commentary,* March 12, 2008, "FSBO Sellers Decreasing" by Jessica Lautz, Research Staff, National Association of Realtors, 430 N. Michigan Avenue, Chicago, IL. See also "Field Guide to Working with FSBOs: Most Important Reason for Selling

Home as FSBO," where 27% sold to a relative or friend and 14% had the buyers directly contact them, as noted at http://www.realtor.org/library/library/fg2109. Accessed on October 9, 2009. The percentage dropped slightly to the 37% figure I mention here where 26% sold to a relative/friend/neighbor and 11% had the buyer contact them directly. See http://www.realtor.org/library_secured/library/fg210 as accessedAugust 12, 2010.

25. Realtor®Magazine Online: A FSBO Conversion Guide at http://www.realtor.org/rmotoolkits.nst/pages/rsbo00/. See "Component 7, Handout 3: 10 Free Things FSBOs Want," Accessed August 12, 2010.

26. According to NAR, "The median selling price of an open-market FSBO home was $185,000, while the median price for all agent-assisted sales was $215,000." This is better than 15% more for the agent-assisted sale. Data is updated as of March 12, 2010. See http://www.realtor.org/press_room_secured/public_affaird/tpfsbo. Accessed August 11, 2010.

27. "Profile of Home Buyers and Sellers, 2000," *National Association of Realtors*, October 2008.

28. Obviously, I am not recommending what they should be, only that a premium service and premium expertise deserve a premium commission and represent excellent value for the consumer.

29. See Note 20.

30. I consult for high end sellers, developers and agents on market positioning, pricing, and *power marketing*. See http://PowerMarketing.pro.

31. For an example of such a quarterly market report go to "Free Stuff" on my website, http://PowerMarketing.pro.

32. As throughout the book here, too, I have used writer's license to reconstruct dialogue that tries faithfully to convey the point of the conversation.

33. I have created a sample generic marketing plan that can be purchased along with the 12 Business Essentials of Every Listing Agreement at http://PowerMarketing.pro. It can then be adapted to your individual use.

34. "Code of Ethics and Standards of Practice of the National Association of Realtors," National Association of Realtors, January 1, 2010.

35. Bacon, *Essays*, "Of Delays," p. 64.

36. Thomas Hobbes observed "That which takes away the reputation of love is being detected of private ends." *Leviathan,* p. 102.
37. Hobbes, *Leviathan,* p. 86.
38. Leo Strauss, *The Political Philosophy of Thomas Hobbes* (Chicago: University of Chicago Press, 1932), p. 11.
39. Ibid., p. 11.
40. This is a constant theme throughout the founding of modern liberal democratic thinking. See John Locke's *Second Treatise of Government,* and the *Federalist Papers* written by Alexander Hamilton and James Madison.
41. As Bacon advised "nature will lay buried a great time, and yet revive upon the occasion or temptation," *Essays,* "Of Nature in Men," Francis Bacon, p. 113.
42. Hobbes, *Leviathan,* p. 64.
43. Bacon, *Essays,* "Of Great Place," p. 33.
44. Bacon, *Essays,* "Of Great Place," p. 29.
45. Bacon, *Essays,* "On Adversity," p. 16.
46. Hobbes, *Leviathan,* p. 105.
47. Hobbes, *Leviathan,* p. 141.
48. I am creating one now and it will appear on my website, http://PowerMarketing.pro.

Index

Made in the USA
Middletown, DE
29 January 2025

70475446R00146